HOW TO GIVE
Successful Parties

HOW TO GIVE
Successful
Parties

Stephen and Nicky Adamson

SMITHMARK

This edition published in 1991 by Paul Hamlyn Publishing,
part of Reed International Books Limited,
Michelin House, 81 Fulham Road, London SW3 6RB

First published in the United States by
SMITHMARK Publishers Inc.,
112 Madison Avenue, New York, NY 10016

SMITHMARK books are available for bulk purchase for
sales promotion and premium use. For details write or telephone the
Manager of Special Sales, SMITHMARK Publishers Inc.,
112 Madison Avenue, New York, NY 10016 (212) 532 6600

© Reed International Books Limited 1991

ISBN 0 831 7-4660-2

Produced by Mandarin Offset – printed in China

CONTENTS

INTRODUCTION

According to the Ancient Greeks, man is a sociable animal. Certainly, nearly all of our enjoyment comes through the company other people, and even a gourmet meal or a hilarious film is not half the fun on our own. Therefore, when we want to celebrate, we get together with others. Whether there is some special event or we just want to have a good time, the way to do it is to throw a party.

Like people, parties come in many different shapes and sizes. When we are young a party is ice cream, cake and games. In youth it is a lot of friends getting together in the evening with drink, food and possibly music. But then comes the age of discrimination, and with it a widening of possibilities. A party can now be a small number of people coming round for dinner, a family get-together on an anniversary, a troupe of different age groups heading for a picnic in the hills, or all your friends assembling to see how high they can raise the roof.

The art of giving a successful party lies in making the right decisions. Of course, you have to know the questions before you can come up with the answers, so the emphasis is always on thinking ahead and being prepared. If you are tense because you are still worrying about what you have to do, this will communicate itself to your guests. To make sure everyone enjoys themselves, arrange things so that you can have a good time yourself – then go for it!

Food and drink are important to the success of any party, but there is one ingredient that is absolutely essential, and that is good company.

The first decision is to settle on the type of party you want to give. Size is a determining factor – eight makes a good number for a dinner party, but will scarcely do for cocktails. But once you have decided on the approximate numbers, there are many options to consider.

Your first assumption might be that parties happen indoors, but perhaps it's the summer and you should use the back yard, patio or poolside. Maybe you should go out completely and have a picnic at a local beauty spot. Evenings are the most common time for entertaining, but a weekend lunchtime might work better, especially if children are to be included – and any time of day from breakfast to supper can be pressed into service with its very own style of party. Costume parties, games and special themes are frequent features of children's parties, but they can lift adult parties out of the ordinary too. Or perhaps you don't like having to produce food on a large scale, so an early-evening cocktail party could be the answer.

In any event, have a good look at all the options first, and don't just assume you will do what you have always done. Trying for something a bit different can fire the host and hostess with enthusiasm, and with that precious commodity at the outset you are already three-quarters of the way to giving an excellent party.

Invitations

There is an optimum time for sending out invitations. Leave it too late and people may be booked up already, send them too early and they may get forgotten, or it might look as if you are feeling insecure about people coming. Three to four weeks' notice is usually about right. Put RSVP on the bottom of written invitations and do not feel diffident about phoning people who have not replied within

---

Invitation codes

Three sets of words can be printed in the bottom left hand or bottom right hand corner of an invitation to indicate the formality of dress. Without one of these, either better casual dress or suits for men are equally expected.
- "suits" means that the women should be chic and that the men should wear suits
- "black tie" means cocktail dress for women and tuxedos for men.
- "white tie" indicates "tails", or evening suits, for men and evening dress for women.

---

two weeks. This still gives you time to invite replacements from your reserve list.

The exception to this is wedding receptions, where a much longer period is the norm because it is assumed that everybody invited is an essential guest and so needs plenty of notice to ensure that they are free (and can have good time to buy a present!).

The more formal the invitation, the more formal the event. If you are having a drinks party and invite everybody on the phone, they will expect it to be casual. Likewise, telephone invitations to dinner imply casual dress, while a written one suggest ties and jackets or suits for the men. However, this is by no means a formal convention and if you want people to dress up in any way, you should say so.

Stationers supply ready-printed invitations with blanks for you to fill in. These are quite acceptable even for formal parties; if you have invitations specially printed it indicates that you are going to some expense over the party.

Food for large numbers

While the prominence given to the food will vary tremendously from its being the focus of attention in a dinner party to its secondary role in a cocktail party, it is, nevertheless, an important element of all entertaining. There are various principles that apply equally to the planning and preparation of food in all parties.

The first thing is not to be daunted by numbers. Catering for a lot of people is no more complicated than preparing for a smaller party, it is just that the amount of food provided will increase. The actual number of

dishes can remain the same; doubling the numbers does not mean that you have to double the choice. In fact, the opposite is often the case: You may feel that you will be open-handed in catering to a small group by providing a large array of delicacies, while for a large gathering the sheer volume of just a few dishes will look lavish.

It is crucial to sit down long before the party and write out a list of what you are going to provide. Then shop in advance. You can spread the load with this, as items that keep can be purchased with the normal weekly shopping and stored, leaving only perishables to be bought two days or the day before.

For a large party start the cooking several days in advance; this will not only save you being tired on the day, but enables you to assess the food to check that you are providing enough and that it is well-balanced. What looks good on paper might look deficient in either quantity or variety when it starts to take form in the kitchen. There are many dishes that can go in the freezer, but don't forget to take things out in advance so that your prize dip is not a huge green ice cream when the party starts.

Bringing in professionals

You don't have to stagger home under bales of shopping if you are solvent enough to cook with your checkbook. Catering companies will happily provide all the food you need, precooking it and just doing the finishing touches in your kitchen on the day. These companies often advertise in local newspapers or can be found in the Yellow Pages. Book them well in advance to guarantee availability. They will offer you a selection of foods at different prices, and if worth their salt will be able to advise you on what goes down well.

Buying the food

To make sure that you get everything that you need when you need it, adopt a three-stage list.

- First, list everything you are going to need, copying down the ingredients from recipes and adding fruit, cookies, bread, nibbles and anything else you will provide but not cook.
- From the first list write down all items that can be bought a few days in advance when you normally shop. This is for items that will keep and ingredients for dishes you will cook in advance.
- List three is what is left, which should be things like salad ingredients that have to be bought the day before to guarantee freshness.

There is a half-way house between being a slave to your kitchen or to your bank account, which can work very well for buffets. To save cooking large numbers of quiches or pizzas, get them from caterers while you prepare the salads and desserts. Alternatively, you can order them from pizza houses or delicatessens and pick them up on the day. These establishments usually require less notice than caterers, so are a good standby if you have left things late or find yourself overwhelmed a couple of days before the party.

Caterers will also supply celebration cakes to order. This is often a good way of producing a more elaborate birthday cake for a children's party than you could make yourself with normal kitchen equipment. Not only do

It always pays to take the time to look for good quality ingredients.

they normally have a wide variety of novelty designs at their disposal, but will rise to the challenge of being asked for something really unusual. Often you do not even have to let your fingers do the walking as some moms do a special sideline in making cakes semi-professionally from home.

The green touch

Any environmentally aware party-thrower will consider it worth the extra expense of buying organic fruit and vegetables and free-range eggs both for the lack of harmful side effects and for the improved flavor. These are now available from some supermarkets as well as health-food shops.

Environment-friendly food does not have to be vegetarian, but the production of vegetable protein uses less land than meat. However, if you want to provide meat, small quantities in stews, casseroles and salads show greater environmental concern than large amounts on their own. Look for specialist organic suppliers who sell meat from animals that have been fed on natural products and allowed freedom of movement, and have not been treated with steroids.

The incredible shrinking appetite

For some reason, the more people there are at a function, the less they eat per person. Perhaps this is because we eat more when we are in front of food, and at large parties guests only make occasional forays to a buffet table, or wait for food to come round. Also, the attention is not focused on the food, but on socializing. In preparing recipes for 20 or more people (other than for sit-down meals) allow for them to eat only about three quarters as much per head as they would for dinner. This figure becomes even lower at children's parties, and most parents are familiar with the sight of moms and dads tucking into plates of scarcely touched sandwiches after the children's meal. Even treats like ice cream and cake often seem to be regarded as distractions from the main business of games and running around. But don't lose heart – children still enjoy the presence of these showpieces, even if they don't eat much of them!

Holding your drink

Whatever kind of drink you are providing – whether wine, beer, cocktails or spirits – it is unlikely that you will have enough glasses of your own to cope with any other than a small party. The liquor store you buy the drink from may well let you borrow glasses for nothing, apart from the cost of replacing any breakages. This is something worth considering when weighing up the pros and cons of going to the liquor store or the supermarket. Otherwise they can be rented from professional catering companies.

Liquor stores will also supply beer and wine, and sometimes hard liquor, on sale-or-return, so you can buy more than you think you are going to need, thereby providing a cushion against running out. One of the most common failings at parties is not to provide enough non-alcoholic drinks. Children are the first consideration, and as they get excited they also get thirsty, especially if you are outdoors on a hot day. Then there are the drivers, and whether or not you feel it is up to you to tell people how much they should drink, you are certainly not helping the resolve of those with the car keys by not giving them any alternative to alcohol. Many non-drivers will quite happily have a drink or two but then reach a limit and want to move on to soft drinks. There are also those who simply arrive plain thirsty. Finally, there are those adults who do not drink at all.

Drinks for the non-drinker

Fortunately, the non-drinker is no longer faced with the choice of children's drinks or the faucet. Non-alcoholic beers and wines are almost as available as the genuine article; as are low-alcohol beers, which many people consider have more flavor. The selection of mineral waters is beginning to rival that of whiskey. Another growth area is carbonated fruit drinks, offering more vitamins and less sugar than traditional ones. There are also a lot more fruit juices available. Buy them in large cartons rather than individual ones, which are much more expensive, and decant them into pitchers to avoid overflow from squeezable cartons. If you do leave cartons out for people to help themselves, see that they are easy to open, and if not leave out scissors for guests to use.

The longer a party goes on the greater is the demand for non-alcoholic drinks, and more non-alcoholic drinks will be consumed proportionally at lunchtime than in the evening.

Games

Party games for adults are very much a matter of taste. Some people love them, others squirm

with embarrassment. In the right company they can be a great ice-breaker, but you need to know your guests well to have them. You would need the charisma of a Billy Graham and the organizational ability of a General George S. Patton to get a large party to play games. There are other ways too in which they are better suited to smaller gatherings: you will know all the guests better yourself, and each person can feel that he or she is getting to know the others. Properly organized they can be a great source of fun, though you should know in advance what you want to play, and have any props ready.

With young children it is a different story as games are the major element of parties for them. Plan them carefully, with one or two more up your sleeve than you expect to use in case

some don't go down well. Prop preparation is essential, as some games like Pin the Tail on the Donkey cannot happen without them.

Provide plenty of toys and play equipment as well, for times between games, alternatives, or just for game drop-outs.

Arranging the home

Two considerations determine how you organize your home for large parties, but sadly they often clash. You will want to make the place look as attractive as possible, but you also have to be practical about removing fragile objects from positions where they could be damaged. However much you want to display your antique china over the fireplace, your party will be ruined if a guest elbows a Meissen figurine to the floor. Children's parties demand an even

Carefully provided equipment can be the making of a children's party.

more thorough removal of precious objects, as they are likely to become maelstroms of activity. In some ways, however, the problem is smaller as it can just be a matter of moving things up to a higher point.

Once you have settled on the numbers coming and the type of party, decide which rooms are going to be used. If you feel it necessary, lock any rooms you do not want used, both for security and to set aside areas where you can at least try to forget about it all afterward.

For a large party, especially one with dancing, designate one room as a "sitting out room" where people can recharge their batteries. Make it quiet and restful, well away from the music, and with low lighting and comfortable chairs.

A few days ahead think of all the tasks of cleaning and moving that have to be done, if necessary writing them all down. If you have helpers, split the tasks up among them.

Don't forget the bathrooms! Put out plenty of toilet paper and leave guest towels for people to dry their hands.

The usual system for coats is to set aside one of the bedrooms so that coats can be left on the bed. If it is raining provide plenty of hangers so they can be hung up from doors and rails, and rig up a line or rack over the bathtub for very wet coats to drip into it. Wet umbrellas create a bigger problem, and if there is nowhere suitable in your hall, rest them in the bathtub too.

Accidents
As the saying goes, they will happen, and the more people there

are, the greater the statistical chances. Even if you make plenty of room on table tops, plates and glasses will be abandoned on the floor where they make a minefield for unwary feet. But however thorough your contingencies against them, spills and breakages are likely. Leave the dustpan and brush, kitchen mops and paper towels in accessible places for emergency action.

Clearing up
In these environmentally conscious times your first reaction might be that any party is an ecological disaster, producing an inevitable amount of waste, a lot of dish-washing and throwing away, and piles of empty bottles. But it looks different if you think that all the people at your party would otherwise be eating and drinking anyway. Catering in bulk is less wasteful of resources and energy than catering individually.

One way or another you are going to have lot of cleaning up to do. However, there is one magic word that can make it a lot better, and that is "help". Cleaning up in other people's homes is never the chore that it is in your own. Do not feel that offers of assistance are made purely out of an overdeveloped sense of duty: guests who have had a great time are often only too happy to help afterward, and will liven up the task as they do.

Be logical in the way you do things, and if you do have helpers, delegate so that everyone has a job to concentrate on. The first thing to do is to go around with garbage bags, putting in everything that is to be thrown away, before you start washing dishes. If you have a garden put anything vegetable into a separate

bag, for eventually putting on the compost pile. Return bottles to the cardboard cases you picked them up in for a trip to the bottle bank – this will help alleviate some of the feelings of wastefulness.

Separating empty cans can serve the same function. Try the aluminum test. If they are not attracted by a magnet, then they are aluminum, and can be given to an organization collecting them for recycling. Steel can also be recycled. Return them to your local can bank; there should be one near you.

Finally, resist any temptation to swallow the dregs of bottles. Instead, when you have finished, make yourself your favorite drink, whether tea or tequila sunrise. You have earned it!

Even a formal dinner party does not have to be an unecological extravagance in these green times. Vegetarian food is generally less demanding of the environment than meat, especially if it is organic.

INFORMAL PARTIES

The informal party is the occasion to assemble a good number of people, shake them all together, add a fuse in the form of some drink, and then hope that the whole thing goes off with a bang. It is the time for old friends to meet up again, new friends to be made, and enemies to avoid each other if not to be reconciled!

The rules are few at informal parties, though you can make your own by throwing a costume party. There are no strictures on what to wear and there is no place designated for each person to sit. Good company is their essence, and although as host or hostess, you will be putting a lot of work into preparing food and drink and making your home look attractive, all this is only ancillary to encouraging people to socialize with each other.

Whether the party is indoors or outdoors, lunchtime or evening, what characterizes an informal party is that people are free to move around the other guests as they wish. Circulation is the name of the game, and there should always be enough people at an informal party for guests to be able to move on to talk to somebody else.

For most of us a "party" is an informal party. But that does not prevent there being a thousand and one ways to make each party different, exciting and memorable.

Food at cocktail parties does not have to be substantial but should be arranged to look as attractive and inviting as possible.

Looking after Your Guests

A party is no more than the sum of the people there, and whatever else happens, a good party is simply one where everybody enjoys themselves. To guarantee this calls for both careful advance planning and some work on the night.

Whereas at, say, a formal dinner party, people will make an effort to get along with the person sitting on each side, the openness and fluidity of the informal party means that care has to go into making sure that guests are likely to be in company they enjoy. Thinking of this starts when you first consider whom to invite.

The guest list
When drawing up the guest list you may be tempted just to ask as many people as you can fit into the rooms available – or more, because about 10–25 percent of those invited will not be able to make it, especially at busy times like Christmas. Inviting *all* your friends is usually a guarantee of success, as everyone is bound also to be friendly with at least some of the other people there. However, space and expense may force you to be more selective, and this calls for thought to be given to the balance of people. Apart from extreme extroverts, most people like parties where there is a mix of those they know

With all the preparation out of the way, the host's or hostess's main function during the party is to make sure that everyone is enjoying themselves and that nobody gets to feel left out.

and those they don't. This creates the opportunity of getting to know new people, with a good bank of old friends to enjoy and to fall back on.

If you are inviting people who will know no one else, or very few other people, think of which other guests will have something in common with them, and then fix this in your mind so that you make sure you introduce them to each other. The first few minutes can drag terribly for anyone left on their own or finding themselves with someone with whom conversation is hard work.

Absent friends
As for the age-old problem of friends you have not invited, there is no simple answer. In practice this is much more of a problem in the host's mind than anywhere else, as most friends who get to hear that there is a party to which they have not been invited will shrug it off. Often there is a reason for being selective, and you can let people know what it is. Perhaps the party is mainly for work associates; in this case the best thing is to drop casually into conversation with other friends that you are having to give this special party, and maybe even that you find it a bit of a chore.

Making introductions
As host or hostess you have to make sure you will have time to circulate and introduce guests to each other.

Even when everything seems to be going full swing and you might feel that it is finally time to pour yourself a drink, some guests might be stranded with somebody they don't really like. A good host or hostess will recognize signs of boredom or irritation, and whisk off the suffering party with some remark like "I know you two are getting along famously, but I must just take John over to meet Charles, because I know Charles will never forgive me if I don't." However, if you find that you are still placing olives on canapes, cleaning glasses or mixing fruit cups when your guests have started arriving,

then you won't be able to do this all-important job of effecting introductions. The start of the party can be the trickiest time in this respect because it is the time when you are going to have most on your mind. What am I going to do with the coats? When should we serve the first tray of food? Is the wine at the right temperature? Are all the mixers at hand? Have I put out all the ashtrays? To avoid being distracted by all these, write a checklist a couple of days beforehand of things to do on the day and make sure that everything has been done – apart from last minute heating of food – well before the guests are due.

Planning ahead

Decide on the following at least a couple of days ahead:
- how and when to rearrange the furniture
- what you are going to wear
- when you are going to buy flowers and how many
- how many ashtrays you are going to need, and whether to buy or borrow any extra
- where you will put the food, plates, cutlery and glasses
- which room the coats will be put in, and whether it is suitable if they are wet
- when to start chilling wines
- what time you will start circulating the food.

The Drinks

The basis of any informal party is the drink, and it is going to be a major expense. In general, the larger the party, the less critical attention the guests will pay to what they are drinking, but careful thought still has to go into the choice. The secret is in providing the best possible quality within your budget.

The basic outline of what you are going to provide is already determined if you announce a cocktail party, a wine and cheese party or a sherry party, and you can then get down to details. The smaller the party, the easier the choice is, too, because you are more likely know whether you are inviting a posse of hardened beer drinkers or a clutch of wine connoisseurs. But for most parties, some sort of balance is called for.

Wine

Wine has many advantages as the basic drink for the straightforward informal party. There are many perfectly decent inexpensive wines, so it need not cost a fortune. Wine is easy to serve, and you need only to go around refilling glasses with a bottle of red in one hand and a bottle of white in the other. Wine can also be put out on the drinks table for people to help themselves while you get on with other things or with talking to your guests. Wine also can be mixed with soft drinks and hard liquor to make punches. Finally, wine is not heavily alcoholic, so you run less risk of knocking guests out. Note that white wines are less strong than red ones, and

Rieslings less alcoholic than Chardonnays.

However, wine does have its disadvantages, the main one being that not everybody likes it. It is therefore usually necessary to provide some alternative such as beer, in addition to non–alcoholic drinks, which can be left on the drinks table for people to help themselves. Red wine stains terribly, and swift action is necessary if it gets spilt.

Red wine stains

If red wine gets spilled on your carpet or tablecloth:
- act quickly
- pour mineral water on the stain
- soak up wine and water with paper towels
- sprinkle salt on the area.

Wine no longer comes only in bottles; you can buy jug wine and some places now sell it in vacuum-sealed boxes. The main advantage of these boxes is that the wine in it keeps well after it has been opened – though this is not likely to be a major consideration at a large party. Boxes contain three or four bottles' worth, so they save on time in pulling corks, and they are

less likely to be knocked over or to spill badly if they are. The drawbacks with them are that you cannot go around refilling glasses straight from a box, and the tap will drip on to your table or floor if it is not turned off fully every time, so you need to place a receptacle below it.

Generally more white wine than red is drunk at parties, in the ratio of two to one, especially at lunchtime; always provide both.

Allow three glasses of wine per head on average, with a good reserve for a long party. Expect to get six glasses of wine per bottle.

Chilling white wine

If the refrigerator is already too full to take more than a few bottles, buy two big bags of ice, from a supermarket or liquor store. Two hours before the party put one bag in the refrigerator and the ice from the other into a large plastic container, such as a clean trash can. Put in as many bottles as will fit, and top up with cold water.

Replace the bottles you take out, and when all the ice in the bucket has melted, pour in the contents of the bag from the refrigerator.

Stand the bucket on a plastic

sheet or on a water-resistant floor surface to catch spills.

Other drinks

Unless you want strictly to stick to a single type of drink, it is a good idea to provide at least some beer. There will be some guests that do not care for wine or cocktails, and there will also be those who are just thirsty. The amount you need to provide will be determined by knowing your guests; if you are asking the local football club around, the white wine is not likely to be seriously touched, but think of the amount

Wine is popular for party drink, but it does not have to be served neat. For a summer buffet it can be made into a fruit cup as here, where red wine has been mixed with brandy, soda water, sugar, lemon slices and mint.

of beer they will drink and double it! Beer drinkers do not like their drink warm, so if you have a bucket of iced water for the wine, put some cans in as well.

At most cocktail parties the drinks offered are simple mixed drinks – highballs, gin or vodka and tonic, and so on. The usual way of serving these – unless the party is very small – is to place all the bottles, including the mixers, and an ice bucket (frequently replenished) on the sideboard or bar and station someone there to pour the drinks. If the room is very crowded, the host or hostess, or a waiter or helper, should circulate with drinks.

Non-alcoholic drinks

Quite a lot of people do not drink alcohol at all, there may be children at the party, and there are

certainly those who are driving home. It is easy to underestimate the demand for non-alcoholic drinks, and it has even been known for the host to find withering flowers in emptied vases the next morning! If anything, err on the side of over-generosity in supplying cartons of fruit juice, bottles of mineral water, and giant-size plastic bottles of soft drinks. Providing they have not been opened, most of these will keep almost indefinitely, so you will get round to using the left-overs eventually. You may know all your guests and their drinking habits well and be able to work out how much of each they are likely to drink. If not, assume that everybody will have one glass of one of these, and that up to a quarter of the guests will drink nothing else.

Cocktail Parties

The cocktail party is the most basic and widespread form of all parties. The beauty of this sort of occasion is its flexibility – it can happen at lunchtime, in the early evening or over the whole evening, and can be as dressy or as casual as you like.

The term "cocktail" party can conjure up images of high living and sophisticated people with long cigarette holders. But a cocktail party is any party in which mixed drinks are served. Even without the term on the invitation, all parties are cocktail parties at which the drink is more important than the food, and in which guests are expected to stand and circulate for much of the time. Most of us have attended scores of cocktail parties, even if they weren't called that.

The cocktail party is the perfect occasion for bringing together lots of people, many of whom won't know each other, and getting them to mix, making new acquaintances and enjoying the company of old ones.

Cocktails

A true cocktail party is a glamorous affair. It is an occasion at which guests feel the need to put on a show. For the men this is chance to get out the white tuxedo or their latest designer-label jacket. The women will get a special dress out of the closet, or if they are lucky a new one from a shop. Traditionally this is "a little black number", though anything that looks chic without being showy or too formal is right. The true cocktail party is an early evening affair. It is a prelude to dinner, so the only food items are small, enough to keep the wolf from the door and to provide blotting paper to stave off inebriation. To invite people to this sort of party written, printed invitations are essential – though ready printed cards with spaces for you to fill in the details are quite acceptable. The important thing is that the

Finishing touches

The final glory of any cocktail is provided by the decoration, and there are plenty to choose from:

- maraschino or glacé cherries
- lemon, lime, orange and pineapple slices
- plain or stuffed green olives
- citrus twists on the side of the glass
- petite parasols used as swizzle sticks or just to prettify the drink
- celery leaves or sticks, pared cucumber peel, pared orange or lemon peel or sprigs of herbs, for tall drinks
- sprigs of mint for mint juleps
- ground spices like cinnamon and nutmeg for dusting sweet, pale-colored cocktails.

invitation must state "cocktails", either in the form of "You are invited to cocktails at…", or in the bottom left or right hand corner. This is the signal to dress up.

The invitations should also give the finishing time, as well as the starting time, for example "5–7pm". As your guests will be dining afterward, they may be eating out and should know what time to reserve the table.

Although people are generally pleased to be served the standby mixed drinks or wine, you can can an extra fillip to your party by offering one or more cocktails. Many cocktails, however, only look right in cocktail glasses, so if you do not have enough of your own, rent them, or stick to the taller drinks that can be served in tumblers.

Most cocktails are strong. They contain at least one kind of liquor, and sometimes two or more. This is why they are suitable for the early evening party, where guests are not going to be there long enough to drink large amounts. If you are going to serve them at an extended party, you need to bear in mind the effect that they will have on your guests' heads, and on your pocket! Rather than have them flow all evening, you could use them to get the party started, and then go on to offering a range of other drinks.

There is no need to offer guests a choice of more than two types of cocktail, and it is perfectly acceptable to offer only one. However, in that case it is best to stick to one of the tried and tested varieties as the more exotic ones are less likely to appeal to everybody.

Of the various classic cocktails, the Manhattan, the Martini, the Tom Collins and the Screwdriver are among the best known and most popular for the early evening. For perfect cocktails measure the quantities precisely using a jigger or shot glass, which contains 1 fluid ounce.

Manhattan

SERVES 6

8 jiggers red vermouth
16 jiggers bourbon whiskey
6 dashes Angostura bitters

Shake the ingredients well with ice and strain into cocktail glasses.

Martini

SERVES 6

12 jiggers gin
12 jiggers dry vermouth

Shake the ingredients well with ice and strain into cocktail glasses.

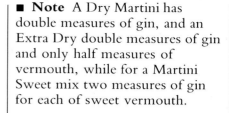

■ **Note** A Dry Martini has double measures of gin, and an Extra Dry double measures of gin and only half measures of vermouth, while for a Martini Sweet mix two measures of gin for each of sweet vermouth.

Tom Collins

SERVES 6

24 jiggers gin
9 teaspoons fine granulated sugar
juice of 3 lemons
soda water

Shake the gin, sugar and lemon juice well with ice and strain into tall tumblers. Add ice and a good dash of soda water to each.

Screwdriver

SERVES 6

24 jiggers vodka
1 quart orange juice

Pour the vodka over ice cubes in each tumbler and fill up with approximately four times as much orange juice. Stir well.

For the individual touch, invent your own cocktail. Be sure, though, to try it out on several people before serving it at a party.

The "Bring-a-bottle" party
Customs have changed somewhat in relation to the party where guests are asked to bring a bottle to drink. It used once to be the domain of the young, but as this generation has grown older the habit of taking a bottle to a party has stuck. The general guideline is that if you actually ask people to bring their own bottles to a

The Martini family. From left to right, Extra Dry Martini, Dry Martini, Martini and Sweet Martini.

party, then it should be very informal indeed, with only basic food and a casual air to the whole thing. However, you may find that some guests bring bottles to the party anyway, even if not asked. Plan on the assumption that you are providing all the drink and regard any bottles left over as thank-you presents from your guests.

Food

Snacks are essential for the cocktail party, but you don't have to provide anything more substantial. If you are having a full-scale evening-long cocktail party, on the other hand, then you do need to provide something more in the way of a meal, and you should look at the buffet section in the next chapter. The variety of snacks you provide is entirely up to you, but do bear in mind that if you offer a large variety of foods, you are making a lot of work for yourself. On the other hand, guests ought to have half a dozen different tasty things on offer if they are to be impressed by your catering.

Do not expect them to consume vast amounts of food; after all, a cocktail party is a pre-dinner occasion. An allowance of two open-face sandwiches and three or four smaller items such as canapes per person should be enough.

Most of the food preparation can, and should, be done in advance. With a freezer, pie shells and the flour and fat for pastry can be made days in advance and frozen (take them out in enough time to defrost). You can also buy ready-made frozen pastry – a great time-saver, if more expensive than making it yourself. Slices of citrus fruits such as lemons or oranges can also be frozen, provided you place them first on freezer paper.

Make your sandwiches the night before and keep them in the refrigerator, wrapped in plastic wrap. Beware, however, of letting the bread become soggy as a result of moist fillings; the way around this is to spread the bread well with butter before adding the filling.

Alternatively, if the sides of

Snacks

While your impulse may be to produce food that you have made yourself, do not forget the prepared and packet snacks. The following always go down well, and do not require much more work than opening a packet and finding an attractive bowl:

- cashew nuts, dry-roasted and salted peanuts, toasted almonds, pecans
- stuffed olives, green or black olives, gherkins
- saltines, English water biscuits, cheese crakers, Triscuits, Bath Olivers, prawn crackers
- spicy proprietary mixes or party-snack mix
- potato chips – a variety of flavors to choose from, but plain salted remain the safe choice.

---

the refrigerator are already bulging, early on the day of the party make open-face sandwiches on firm bases such as toast, butter them well, cover with plastic wrap (making sure it is

---

A LEMON PIG FOR THE FOOD TABLE

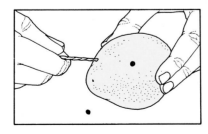 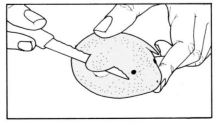 

1 Make a hole on either side of the pointed end of a lemon about a half inch in from the point, using a skewer. Fill each of theses holes with a peppercorn to serve as eyes.

2 Cut a flap on either side of the lemon in towards the middle from the "eyes" with a sharp knife to make the ears.

3 Insert cocktail stick halves for the legs and a parsley stalk in a small hole for the tail.

For a larger pig, the same shape can be made with a firm grapefruit or an orange.

not touching any cheese) and store them in a cool place.

Most dips can be made earlier in the day and left in the refrigerator, as can the vegetable pieces to use with them.

When storing the prepared foods keep those with a strong smell, such as gherkins or onions, well away from the milder foods like cream cheese, or you are likely to find that the blander foods have been tainted with the taste of the powerful ones.

Dips

Dips are great cocktail party favorites. A dip is a non-sweet item, soft enough to stick a small biscuit or raw vegetable into, and firm enough to cling to it without dropping off or making it soggy. With the use of blenders and the widespread availability of cream cheeses and natural yogurts, almost any vegetable and many meats and fish can be the basis of a dip.

However, you have to bear in mind the appearance as well as the taste: a brown mush is easily produced but rarely eaten.

The following three dips are sure-fire successes and not hard to make.

Avocado and cheese dip

SERVES 10

2 tomatoes
2 cloves garlic
onion
2 avocados
1 tablespoon lemon juice
2 oz soft cheese
salt and pepper

Skin, seed and chop the tomatoes. Crush the garlic and grate the onion. Peel the avocados and remove the stone. Mash the avocado flesh with the lemon juice, then beat in the remaining ingredients with a fork or mix them in the blender. Add salt and pepper to taste.

Early evening cocktail parties allow you to entertain in style without providing vast amounts of food.

Smoked mackerel dip

SERVES 10

1 medium-sized smoked mackerel
fillet
1 garlic clove
4 tablespoons sour cream
grated rind of lemon
1–2 tablespoons lemon juice
paprika
salt and pepper

Remove the mackerel flesh from the skin and mash it thoroughly. Crush the garlic and beat it into the mashed mackerel with a fork, and then also beat in the sour cream, lemon rind, salt and pepper and one tablespoon of lemon juice. If the mixture is too firm, add more lemon juice as necessary.

Lemon mayonnaise dip

SERVES 12

cup cream cheese
8 tablespoons mayonnaise
1 cup natural yogurt
grated rind of 1 lemon
2 tablespoons chopped fresh chives
2 teaspoons mint sauce
salt and pepper

Take the cream cheese out of the refrigerator to let it soften. Then mix all the ingredients in the blender until of an even consistency, and season to taste.

■ **Note** Serve dips with small crackers or crudités such as cucumber slices, cauliflower florets, pieces of celery, carrot sticks, sliced mushrooms and zucchini sticks.

Hot food

While finger food should obviously not be too hot to touch, it does not always have to be cold. The limitation on hot food is that it is going to be eaten without a fork, and that means producing items that come in an edible container or that can be skewered on a toothpick. Vol-au-vents and small tomatoes make ideal containers for sauces containing meats, shellfish or vegetables; the following two recipes give an idea for each.

Chicken and ham vol-au-vents

20 frozen vol-au-vent cases
chicken stock cube
2 tablespoons butter
2 tablespoons all-purpose flour
1¼ cups milk
6 oz cooked ham
6 oz cold cooked chicken
2 tablespoons heavy cream
salt and pepper

Bake the vol-au-vent cases as instructed on the package.

Crush the stock cube. Melt the butter, stir in the flour and stock cube and cook gently for 2 minutes, stirring continuously.

Remove pan from heat and gradually add milk. Return to heat and bring slowly to the boil, stirring constantly, until sauce thickens. Then allow it to cool, and add the other ingredients. Mix thoroughly.

Remove cooked cases from the oven. Lift the tops with a sharp knife and set aside. Press the center of the cases down, add the filling, and replace the tops. Warm before serving.

Stuffed cherry tomatoes

½ cup onion
4 oz finely ground beef
1 tablespoon olive oil
1 garlic clove
2 tablespoons chopped basil
2 tablespoons chopped parsley
2 teaspoons chopped thyme
salt and pepper
1 cup breadcrumbs
25 cherry tomatoes
lemon juice
Tabasco sauce
4 tablespoons butter

Chop the onion finely. Fry the ground beef in the oil until it has

GARNISHING WITH CUCUMBERS AND GHERKINS

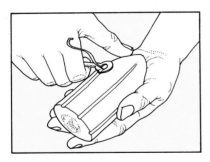

1 Use a canelle knife to remove evenly spaced strips.

2 Cut the striped cucumber into thin, even slices.

1 Slice through a gherkin at regular intervals, but not cutting it as far as the base.

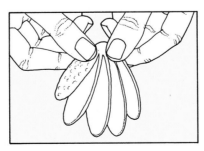

2 Gently pull out the slices so as to make the gherkin into a fan.

just browned, then add the onion and cook until soft. Crush the garlic and mix it with the beef and onions. Mix in the herbs. Season with salt and pepper, and cook gently for a few minutes. Mix in the breadcrumbs and remove from heat.

Cut the tops off the tomatoes. Scoop out the seeds and juice, season the insides and add a squeeze of lemon juice and a dash of Tabasco to each. Fill them with the stuffing and replace the tops.

Grease a dish with butter, put the tomatoes in and cook them at 400°F for 10 minutes. Remove them from the oven and allow them to cool until they are tepid before serving.

Open-face sandwiches

Open sandwiches are ideal for cocktail parties. Not only can you make an interesting-looking spread in each one, but guests can see exactly what it is they are getting! Vary the bread that you use for the bases, choosing from any of the following: white, brown, French, rye, Swedish bread, or finger rolls split in half and used separately. Spread them with butter, covering the bread well if you are making them in advance, so as to stop the filling soaking through. Then place a slice of one of the cheeses on top of the butter and select a topping and one or more garnishes. Look for those that will both complement the taste of the cheese you have chosen and provide a contrast in color.

Arrange the sandwiches in patterns on large plates. For example, if you are using finger roll halves, display them like the spokes of a wheel. Separate the sandwiches with garnishes of cucumber slices, tomato quarters and sprigs of parsley.

Finishing touches

With finger food, presentation starts when you first slice the bread for open-face sandwiches and ends with a choice of garnishes. Finely cut chives, chopped parsley, and leaves from the head of celery all make attractive garnishes to most cocktail party snacks.

Little "bouquets" of watercress made by trimming the ends of a small bunch fairly short, can be arranged around the edges of a plate to give it a fresh, inviting appearance.

Garnish platters of food with slices of citrus fruit, vegetables, gherkin fans and carrot rolls — paper thin lengths of carrot held together with toothpicks.

Clockwise from left: *Snow peas with shrimps, savory scones with cheese, cold savory omelettes with prosciutto and melon, and cherry tomatoes stuffed with meat and basil.*

CHEESES: Cheddar, Monterey Jack, Edam, Gouda, Emmenthal, Gruyère, Jarlsberg, Limburger, Mozzarella, Danish Blue, cottage cheese, cream cheese.

TOPPINGS: sliced cold meats, salami, pâté, chicken, sardines, shrimps, smoked salmon.

GARNISHES: onion rings, parsley, cucumber twists, watercress, tomatoes, cocktail gherkins, olives, hard-boiled eggs, red pepper slices, shredded lettuce, caviar or lumpfish roe, pineapple chunks, orange slices.

Barbecues

There is something irresistible about food cooked out of doors. Ingredients take on an aroma and flavor quite different from when cooked on a stove. The cooking itself is a social event, with guests able to join in and excited children watching the proceedings. For once the cook is at the center of events instead of being tucked away in the kitchen.

You probably won't be planning a barbecue party unless you already own a barbecue, but don't just assume that it is going to be adequate to the task. Some of the standard models are big enough for the average family, but will scarcely feed 30 or 40 hungry people. Do your sums well in advance so that you can arrange to borrow another one from a friend if necessary.

The other basics are pretty straightforward – plenty of fuel, lighting fuel or kindling, tongs, long-handled cooking forks, oven gloves and a sprinkler. If you are cooking in the late evening you will need a flashlight, lamp or candles too.

Positioning the barbecue

After safety considerations, the next concern when positioning a barbecue is that it should be sheltered from strong breezes, and that there is enough space around it for people to stand and chat or join in the cooking. Finally, whereas the smell of burning charcoal is delicious out of doors, it does not have the same romantic feel to it in the bedroom, so position the barbecue well away from doors and open windows – your neighbors' as well as your own.

Preparing the food

Advance preparation is even more necessary with barbecues than with parties indoors. One of the hosts is going to be chained to the barbecue itself for the first half of the party, with the added disadvantage of not having all the usual kitchen utensils immediately at hand. Prepare a space by the barbecue, or put up a portable table, and lay out all the plates, bowls and cooking utensils that you are likely to need. Make sure that you have foil, to prevent

Safety

- Position the barbecue well away from trees, shrubs and wooden buildings, especially if the weather has been dry.
- Keep it away from any routes people will have to take.
- Keep a well-filled sprinkler at hand to douse down excessive flames.
- Never use more lighter fluid than recommended by the manufacturer.
- Don't stand directly over the barbecue, even to check food.
- Keep children at a respectful distance.
- Don't carry a lighted barbecue.

food from burning or falling apart. Cut up all the meat, fish and poultry well in advance. Marinate meat overnight to bring out its fullest flavor and tenderness. Beanburgers should be started the previous day. Prepare salads earlier in the day and keep them fresh under plastic wrap.

Barbecued food can be very simple, one of the reasons being that the flavor of the smoke will impose its character on whatever is cooked. However, there are plenty of dishes that are not unnecessarily fussy to add to the traditional hot dogs, hamburgers and chicken thighs. Cubes of meat, vegetables and fish on skewers cook well and quickly, and can be served with different sauces. Pickles and relishes come into their own as accompaniments because their flavors are strong enough to make an impression through the smoke. Try cucumber relish, apple chutney, or piccalilli – and don't forget the dill pickles.

A selection of salads is all you need to accompany barbecued meat. However, if you can make a potato dish in the kitchen it is a great bonus, as with this potato gratin served with stuffed tomatoes and barbecued chicken breasts and pork chops.

Branching out too far into unusual dishes, though, may disappoint some of the guests, especially children, who will have been looking forward to barbecue standards. One of these makes a good standby to your more exotic offerings.

A good selection of salads is far preferable to trying to prepare cooked vegetables, and is quite appropriate for the warm fine weather you will have been expecting. They are, however, not so popular with children, for whom you could heat up baked beans in an old pan on the fire.

Ice cream and watermelon are the perennial favorites for dessert at a barbecue. A huge bowl filled with chunks of different melons, peaches, blueberries or whatever fruit is in season is a treat for the eye and palate.

Setting the scene

The food can so dominate your thinking in planning a barbecue that other matters get overlooked. Think of where you are going to serve the food – straight from the barbecue is likely to be both impractical and unsafe – and don't forget to put out the plates, cutlery and paper napkins. Thought also has to be given as to where it will be eaten and chairs made available. If you have, or can lay your hands on, a selection of small tables, consider arranging the chairs around them and putting a candle on each – the soft light will add intimacy and warmth to the proceedings. Patio lights can be harsh; backyard torches stuck into flowerbeds are a romantic alternative. The last thing you may want to think about, but not the last think you *should* think about, is what to do if the weather decides to spoil your party. Work out exactly what you

---

Countdown

The day before:
- Buy the food, drink and fuel.
- Marinate the meat.
- Soak beans for vegetarian burgers.

The morning before:
- Make salads.

The afternoon before:
- Prepare the room and yard.
- Set up the barbecue.

One hour before:
- Light the barbecue.
- Set out plates and cutlery.
- Mix the fruit punch, if being offered. Put drinks that should be chilled in the refrigerator.
- Prepare all the foods to be cooked, and cover them.

---

will do about the food and guests should the heavens open.

In choosing drinks, various conflicting demands come into play. As you are probably serving meat, red wine might seem the right choice. On the other hand, if it is a hot evening, white or rosé wine or beer might seem to be more appropriate. Some people swear by hard cider, as an adaptable, thirst-quenching drink.

Think of fish

Fish broils well on barbecues, but it does have a tendency to break up over the intense heat. Stick to whole fish such as trout or mackerel and cook it on a rack 4 to 5 inches fixed above the charcoal, wrapped in foil or held in a special fish broiler. A good alternative is a seafood kebab. Barbecued shrimps are delicious, but need frequent turning to prevent them from burning, and firm fleshed white fish cut up well into small chunks. Avoid flaky fish that will come apart.

Vegetarian choice

A barbecue party used to be a vegetarians' nightmare, but it is now quite possible to make good vegetarian substitutes. The thing to watch for with a beanburger is that the mixture is thick enough to hold together when cooking.

Vegetarian Burger

SERVES 10–12

2 cups presoaked beans (red, kidney or haricot beans)
3 medium onions, chopped
2 garlic cloves, crushed
1/2 cup mushrooms, chopped
2 tablespoons chopped parsley, basil, thyme or sage
4 cups breadcrumbs
salt and pepper
4 medium eggs
3 tablespoons vegetable oil

Drain the beans and cook in boiling water until soft (about 40 minutes). If you are using kidney beans first boil them fiercely for 15 minutes to destroy any toxins. Fry the garlic and onions in the oil until soft, add the mushrooms and continue frying until done. Mix in a bowl with the herbs (use any combination), and breadcrumbs, and season. Mash the beans thoroughly, then add them to the vegetables. Break the eggs and mix them in one by one.

If the mixture is too wet, add more breadcrumbs or wholewheat flour. If it won't bind together, stir in another egg. Shape into burgers with floured hands. Baste with a little oil when cooking.

A barbecue is a perfect way of cooking kebabs. These chunks of white fish (right) were marinated in yogurt, olive oil and peppercorns before cooking, while the beef has been broiled with onions and mushrooms.

Picnics

A picnic is one of the most delightful way of entertaining friends, as you can go to the romantic, impressive or exciting setting of your choice. Because all the work has to be done in advance, you can relax and enjoy yourself too.

An all-adult picnic can be a very elegant affair, with chilled wines, pâtés and terrines brought in sealable plastic containers, cold soups from vacuum flasks, cooked meats in fine sauces, a selection of salads, and to top it off, a robust and spicy cake.

This kind of fare is perfect for a long lazy afternoon, but you will need to bring a large number of plates, cutlery and glasses. You are not likely to be content with serving a galantine, say, on paper plates with plastic forks.

Picnics, however, are wonderful for families, when a more informal air reigns. It is better for these to provide food that can mainly be eaten with the fingers. Some forks will probably still be necessary, but here lightweight plastic ones will not seem at all out of place.

Food
Slice quiches or meat loaf into small portions, fill buns with slices of cold meat and lettuce or with sloppy dips like taramasalata or houmous, and stuff rolls with cheeses and cucumber, cooked meats, or egg salad. Hardboiled eggs (don't forget to bring the salt!), cold sausages, deviled eggs and chicken drumsticks are all easy to prepare and to pack. Accompany all these cooked foods with two or three ready-made salads, packed away in plastic containers. There is no need to neglect the humble sandwich, and it is one of the best forms of food to have for children. Vary the breads on offer or select from the many types and shapes of roll available. Even the sliced white loaf can be made interesting when used in club sandwiches.

Fillings are as varied and exciting as you want them to be. Try a bit of experimenting in advance with unusual combinations: mashed avocado and egg salad, peanut butter with cream cheese and sliced celery, and bacon, spinach and sliced egg have all proved rewarding inventions.

For dessert bring fruit and cakes, though avoid very sloppy ones, or ones oozing jam in the wasp season. Go to town on the cookies – they are easy to carry and are the ultimate finger food.

Drink
Having to carry it all is going to restrict the amount of drink you bring. One or two alcoholic drinks and a supply of mineral water and/or iced tea will satisfy the grown-ups; bring diluted fruit drinks, plastic bottles of carbonated drinks or individual cartons of fruit juice for the children. A white or rosé wine chilled in advance and brought in the cooler tastes lively and refreshing in the open air, or even better is a sparkling wine if the budget runs to it.

Some people like hot drinks to round off the meal, even on a hot day. Black coffee does not keep too badly, but unfortunately, the taste of neither white coffee nor tea is improved by a long stay in a Thermos, so instead fill the flasks with boiling water and bring tea bags, coffee granules and milk so as to make it fresh.

A picnic is an excellent way of entertaining whole families.

Equipment

Picnics call for a lot of equipment:
- cooler
- rugs or old blankets
- hamper, or bags for carrying food and utensils
- plates, glasses (real or plastic), cutlery
- sealable plastic boxes for wet or fragile food
- paper napkins
- straws for children's drinks
- salt and pepper
- bottle-opener, corkscrew
- sharp knives for cutting
- plastic bags for taking rubbish away

Patios and Poolsides

If you are contemplating a summer party, why not have it outside on the patio where you can enjoy the scent of the evening flowers, or by the pool if you have one, so as to enjoy refreshing dips?

With any sort of outside entertaining, one has to take account of the weather. There is the obvious problem of having an alternative setting planned for a summer downpour, but weather has other tricks to play on us.

One problem is wind. A gentle breeze that would scarcely be noticeable if you are walking about makes unpredictable forays on tablecloths and napkins and deposits them where it wishes. Another consideration is how a hot day can sometimes decline into a cool evening once the sun goes down, and suddenly everybody is wishing they had brought sweaters.

If you have attractive garden tables you may not need to cover them at all, but the chances are that you will have to put out folding tables that will benefit from a decorative tablecloth. Nobody need know that the spread is supported by your old decorating table, unless you tell them. Cotton or linen is less likely to blow about than paper, but even these materials can be

While a patio provides a good setting for a drinks party on a warm evening, it can also become an outdoor room for a sit-down dinner. With a little thought and imagination even a plain brick wall can be turned into a smart background.

disturbed by a sudden gust.

If you use paper tablecloths secure them to the top of the table with strips of double-sided tape, or if this might damage a polished surface, wrap the edges of the tablecloth around the table and secure them to the underside with ordinary tape. Proper cloth ones can be anchored to the edge of the tables with special caterers' clips; if you cannot find some, use large stationery clips and make them look less functional with pieces of colored paper tucked round their tops.

Anchor napkins firmly under plates. It is not a good idea to fold them elegantly into glasses, unless you are confident there will be no more than the slightest breeze. Otherwise, paper napkins will be blown out, and cloth ones will act as a sail, with the danger of bringing the glasses crashing to the ground.

Hot summer days are normally followed by very warm nights, except in certain parts of the country; but if the temperature does drop sharply, it's best to move the party indoors so that the festive spirit does not drop too! You can leave the patio doors open for those who prefer to be under the stars.

Patios
Your patio may need no special

preparation; walls bedecked with honeysuckle provide enough delight to the senses on their own. But if not, buy, beg or borrow large pot plants or miniature trees in tubs, or even better in crafted ceramic pots. For lighting, string up colored lights or burn large backyard torches. Neither of these provide enough light on their own, so leave lights on and draperies open in the room adjoining the patio. On a breezy night, put night lights in jars where they won't blow out.

Finally, remember the uninvited guests. Your friends will not recall the party with quite such a rosy afterglow if the next day they find themselves scratching mosquito bites. There are various electrical devices on the market that either repel biting insects, or else attract and then kill

Impromptu patio parties

Just as weather can force an outdoor party indoors, so you can take advantage of unexpectedly good weather and move an indoor party out of doors. If it is impractical to move the food and drink, open up the french doors and scatter floor cushions against patio walls and other firm, flat surfaces; people will soon find their way outside.

Safety tips

- Keep glasses off the poolside. Either use plastic ones or put out tables.
- Don't swim within half an hour of eating — longer for a large meal.
- Always supervise children swimming.
- Have a non-drinker to supervise any adults who have been drinking.
- Ban all horseplay from the poolside.
- No jumping into crowded pools.

them, or you can buy citronella candles that smell perfectly pleasant to human beings but quite dreadful to mosquitoes.

Parties by the pool

If you have a swimming pool, it makes a wonderful centerpiece for any summer party, whether lunchtime, pre-dinner or evening. Warn the guests in advance that you will be using the pool, so that they can bring their swimsuits and towels. But also have as many spare towels handy as you can, for those who forget their own or who go in the water several times.

Make the pool as much fun as you can, for adults as well as children, with inflatable toys like sharks and crocodiles. You may use the pool yourself mainly for doing healthy laps of front crawl, but even a few people in the average domestic pool do not leave much room for actual swimming, so provide a couple of inflatable balls and rings for them to throw around.

Let your guests know at what time you are going to serve the food, so they can get their watersports in in advance and not find they are digesting when they would rather be dipping. This needs to be made specially clear to any children, as some of them are determined to go in but very reticent when it comes to putting feet in the water, so you don't want to find that a friend's child has finally overcome their reserve after quarter of an hour's struggle, only to be hauled out immediately by a parent because the food has appeared.

Experienced young girl swimmers might enjoy putting on a water ballet for the other guests to watch. This could be planned and rehearsed before the party and put on as an entertainment at some time in the evening.

Food

Outdoor eating on home territory is definitely the time to produce an array of salads. A good salad starts in the shopping; choose fresh, crisp ingredients then combine them in unusual ways or add a herb or some out-of-the-ordinary ingredient to add something a bit different to the flavor. For example, a potato salad becomes all the more interesting with mint and fennel sprigs, and tomatoes take on a new life when combined with basil and chopped green onion.

For combinations, try avocado with endive, lettuce with raw cauliflower florets, cold lightly cooked broccoli in a vinaigrette, or sliced cucumber with *crème fraîche* and lemon juice. There are endless possible permutations; start with whatever ingredients that look good in the shop at the time, as good salad vegetables rarely fail, while no amount of artistry will hide a limp lettuce or overripe tomato.

Salad dressings are vital; a well-made one can transform a good salad into something quite exciting.

The salads are likely to serve as companions to cold meats and fish, but they can be put together in some glorious dishes. The following old English dish dates back in origin at least to the sixteenth century.

LEMON AND CUCUMBER BUTTERFLIES

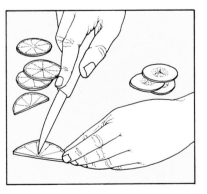

1 Slice a lemon or cucumber thinly. Take each slice and cut it from the edge with a sharp knife.

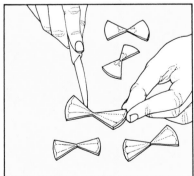

2 Open each slice out from the middle to form a butterfly.

Salamagundy

SERVES 6

1 cold roast chicken
16 small onions, skinned
2 cups green beans
1 × oz can anchovy fillets
4 hard-boiled eggs, shelled and
quartered
1 large lettuce, washed
1¼ cups red grapes, seeded
¼ cup flaked slivered almonds
¼ cup raisins
fresh herbs
vinaigrette dressing

Carve the chicken into slices. Place the onions in a pan of boiling salted water and cook for 10–15 minutes until tender. Drain and leave to cool.

Place the green beans in boiling salted water for 3 minutes until tender. Drain and leave to cool.

Set out all the ingredients attractively on a large platter. Scatter fresh herbs of your preference over them and pour on the vinaigrette dressing.

Desserts
Unlike a barbecue, where the all-pervasive aroma of smoke means that an elaborate dessert might be wasted, guests gathered around the pool or on the patio will appreciate the effort put into rounding the meal off in style. As a summertime occasion, this is the moment for dishes using seasonal fruits: strawberry shortcake, fruit compôtes, layercakes topped with strawberries, raspberries or boysinberries, blueberry cheesecake or a cherry pie. If you have an ice-cream-maker, get it going a couple of days in advance, to make ice creams or sherbets with whatever fruit you have on hand, and then store them in the freezer.

Drink
An emphasis on salads and cold dishes calls for light white wines such as Riesling, a Gewurztraminer or a Chenin Blanc. However, red wines make the basis of some wonderfully refreshing long drinks like Sangria (1 bottle Spanish red wine, 4 jiggers brandy, juice of two lemons, 6 jiggers orange juice and cup sugar) or fruit punches, in which they are combined with fruits and spirits or liqueurs. Selzer or mineral water can be added if you want to make them less strong and more thirst-quenching, and you only need to use an inexpensive wine.

Salamagundy (middle) *served with new potatoes, mint and fennel, and a baked alaska to follow.*

Salad dressings
It is important always to use good ingredients and not be tempted by cheap substitutes, especially with the oil. Oils are produced from various seeds, nuts and beans, and each has its own particular flavor. Unrefined oil tastes better, especially the virgin olive oil made from the first pressing, but is more expensive than refined oils. Use wine, cider or herb-flavored vinegars according to taste.

Brunch

The thought of having to face large numbers of people over breakfast horrifies most of us, but a weekend brunch is another matter. This leisurely buffet starts in late morning and can, if desired, stretch well into the afternoon.

As its name suggests, brunch is a hybrid meal – the first meal of the day, but one that is also meant to keep people going until the evening. The accent is very much on informality, with people eating what they want when they want, and subsiding into the newspapers if they do not feel up to conversation. Accordingly, lay all the food out together for guests to keep helping themselves, while you too can relax, doing no more than having to replenish the occasional hot dish.

Thinking first of the breakfast element, have a selection of breads, muffins, croissants and bagels ready warmed, together with a good array of jams, jellies and honey.

The cooked part of brunch derives from the traditional breakfast of more leisurely times, before cornflakes and ready-sliced toast took over. Even hardened breakfast-refusers can persuade themselves to indulge in these dishes at weekends, perhaps psyching themselves into thinking more of the lunch part of the meal. As appropriate for the numbers of guests, cook whatever quantity and combination you think right from sausages, bacon, scrambled eggs, fried eggs, sautéed potatoes, waffles, or pancakes. Coffee cake, fritter and hot biscuits are other favorite items.

Fruit
When planning, think of brunch as a three-course meal, even though you will serve the "courses" simultaneously, as people will want different things at different times. You therefore need a dessert, although for some people this will be the dish they go for first. This is not a rich cake but fruit: ready sliced or segmented and marinated grapefruit, melon, fresh strawberries, blueberries or a selection of oranges, peaches, and so on. Best of all is to make a

large bowl of fruit cocktail such as the one illustrated below:

Melon cocktail

SERVES 10

1 large Ogen melon
1 large canteloupe melon
3 cups raspberries, hulled
juice of 3 limes
juice of 1 orange
2–3 tablespoons fine granulated sugar (optional)
1–2 tablespoons finely chopped fresh mint

Slice the melons in half, remove the seeds and scoop out the flesh with a melon baller. Place it in a serving bowl. Add the raspberries, pour over the fruit juices and stir well to mix. Sweeten with a little sugar, if desired.

Stir in the chopped mint. Cover with plastic wrap and chill for 1–2 hours before serving or leave overnight in the refrigerator.

Favorite drinks

You don't *have* to serve Bloody Marys with brunch, but they seem to go together like gin and tonic. The essential ingredients are two jiggers of tomato juice to each one of vodka, and a dash of Worcestershire sauce per portion. What you add on top of that is very much a matter of taste: salt

Classic Brunch

Different people have their own idea of what constitutes a first-class brunch. Here is a typical lavish menu:
- freshly squeezed orange juice (no substitutes!)
- scrambled eggs on wholewheat toast *or* bacon, sausage and fried egg "sunny side up" *or* cheese omelette, all with fried potatoes
- hominy grits baked in milk with dollops of butter
- waffles with maple syrup
- corn, wholewheat, blueberry or bran muffins
- warmed bagels, rye bread, wholewheat bread, pumpernickel with strawberry jam, grape jelly and honey
- fresh strawberries or blueberries
- Bloody Mary
- Colombian coffee

and pepper, tabasco, lemon juice, celery salt, and celery heads all have their devotees. The other brunch favorite, and a more refreshing alternative, is Bucks Fizz. This is simply equal parts of orange juice and sparkling white wine, served over ice. It repays using freshly squeezed juice, though vintage champagne might be going just a bit too far!

Whatever you might feel about drinking it side by side with alcohol, coffee should be on offer throughout the party. You may well have been up for hours, but some of your guests will still be wiping the sleep from their eyes at your front door, and will need their shot to get going.

Melon cocktail – fruit is popular with both the health-conscious and those with hungover palates.

Teenage Parties

When children get to their teens, parties take on a new aura. The difficulty for parents is knowing just where to draw the line. Teenagers want to be free to organize things as they wish, but most parents, while respecting this, will feel that they still need to exercise a fair degree of control.

You may get nostalgic about the days when an interesting cake, some novelty sandwiches, potato chips and well-managed games were sufficient to entertain your children and their friends, but when they get into their teens, they are looking for a different sort of party altogether.

Not unreasonably, teenagers expect to be treated as adults. This is fine for the older ones, say for an eighteenth birthday party, but those at the younger end of the age range, however much they protest, cannot just be left to get on with it. On the other hand, an adult party, where most of the people stand around talking with a glass in their hand, strikes the average teenager as a waste of good dance space.

Parental involvement
The first reaction from most teenagers on being told by their parents that if they are going to have a party then they, the parents, are going to be there, is that they would rather not have one at all. But as the date gets nearer, realization dawns of the numbers of people coming and of the responsibility of being in charge of the home when there might be strangers around. Most of them then begin to think that maybe having parents around isn't

such a bad idea after all, providing, of course, you are invisible!

Discretion is the keynote. If you help with serving the food and drink, then you can keep an eye on things to make sure it is going well, without looking as if you are a moral policeman. Then, if you wish, you can slip unobtrusively away.

However, it is better not to slip too far, and to make sure that your son or daughter knows exactly where to reach you. Even with adult parties, it is a sad fact that people sometimes gatecrash for the worst of reasons, and items from the house or the guests' property go missing. Teenagers are more susceptible to this kind of unwanted intruder, if only because the teenage grapevine is so efficient.

Like water, teenage parties will spread until they meet an obstacle; lock up any rooms you do not want used.

Saturday night fever
A party is not a party for teenagers without dancing. Assuming that you are having the party at home, this involves a lot of organization – setting aside a room, taking up the rug, removing the furniture, or pushing it to the walls. At least

there is never any shortage of help, as not only can your children look after this themselves, but they are bound to have friends who will be perfectly happy to spend the afternoon before lending a hand. A finishing time that both the parents and the hosts accept must be agreed in advance

and the guests informed – bear in mind in fixing it that some of them may be relying on being given lifts to get home, and that younger teenagers may be collected by parents. Give neighbors plenty of advance warning, and tell them the finishing time too, so that they know when it is going to be safe to try to get to sleep.

Assess how powerful your own sound system is, and borrow one if necessary. Many domestic stereos perform perfectly adequately at normal listening levels but are not built for volume. Lots of people together make much more noise in conversation than you might expect, and the sound level of the music will have to be high just to be heard. This is not a matter of brain-dead teenagers wanting to deafen everybody; it's just the same if you want music to be heard over a gathering of middle-aged adults!

Leaving a pile of records for people to put on what they want is a guaranteed way to provoke arguments, cover the vinyl with scratches (CDs are at least spared this hazard), and probably lose your prize rarities into the bargain. On the other hand, everybody involved in giving the party can enjoy the build-up over the preceding days by recording tapes of favorite tracks and singles.

To drink or not to drink

In a list of the commonest causes of dispute between teenagers and their parents, drink probably takes third place, only losing out to staying out late and domestic noise levels. With a late teen party you may have no objection to a supply of alcohol being provided, depending on what line you have taken on it hitherto. But remember that however sensible your own children are, there will be some present with weaker heads and possibly weaker wills. It's a rash parent who allows hard liquor, if only for the selfish reason that it is your house and you don't want to be faced the next day with messes that would disgrace the cat. Make it clear to your children that they are

A collection of non-alcoholic cocktails: (from left to right) strawberry milkshake, Caribbean cocktail and peach and apple fizz.

responsible for the cleaning up, and that it is up to them to discourage anyone being stupid.

With young teenagers it is a different story, but you no longer expect them to be happy with orange juice and endless soda drinks. Fortunately, there are now ways of producing drinks that look like adult party fare but without the kick, and the blender can be put to good use making fruit cocktails and milkshakes.

Caribbean cocktail

SERVES 12

*1 inch thick slice of
fresh pineapple, peeled, or
3 pineapple rings, drained
6 bananas
1 cups pint fresh orange juice
1 tablespoon lime juice
30 ice cubes, crushed
6 pineapple rings,
halved (optional)*

Place the pineapple, bananas, orange juice and lime juice in a blender and process them until they are smooth. (Lemon juice can be used instead of limes.)

Share the crushed ice between each of 12 chilled tall glasses and pour in the cocktail. If you want to make it look more exotic decorate the rim of each glass with a piece of pineapple.

Tenderberry

*3 cups strawberries
1 pint grenadine
2 cups heavy cream
1 pint dry ginger ale
ground ginger*

Place the strawberries, grenadine and cream in a blender with some crushed ice and blend until well mixed. Pour into a large pitcher,

add dry ginger ale and stir. Serve in tumblers with a little ginger on each drink.

Fueling the fun

When motivated, teenagers have a lot more energy than their elders, and this has to be considered when planning the food. Provide portable food that can be eaten easily, and as far as possible avoid dishes which have to be eaten with a fork sitting down at a table.

Pre-slice pizzas and quiches into portions that will not fall apart in the hand. Garlic bread, kebabs and chicken drumsticks are all popular and "easy", but also think of dips such as taramasalata, houmous, or guacamole. Don't forget bulk; teenage appetites can be very large, so lay on generous supplies of pre-cut French bread, rolls and cheese.

A large supply of nibbles is essential, and here you *can* fall back on some of the childhood staples that were served at younger parties. Novelty varieties of potato chip or crackers seem to keep their appeal, and are

welcomed with appreciative nostalgia.

For barbecue parties, the standard hamburgers and hot dogs invariably get a good reception, but supplement them with something a bit more interesting, such as spare ribs, served with a spicy barbecue sauce. Greek pitta bread makes a good alternative to rolls for the edible envelopes.

Finally, remember that a lot of teenagers these days are vegetarian, so provide some pizzas or quiches that do not contain meat, and make it clear which ones they are, either by labeling them or putting them all on the same side of the table.

Garlic bread

SERVES 12

*1 large loaf of French bread
1/2 cup butter, softened
2 garlic cloves, crushed
1 tablespoon chopped parsley
salt and pepper*

Start by preheating the oven to 400°F.

Alternatives to home

Just as much fun can be had at a teenage party if it is held in a rented room or hall, and you do not then have the worry of what will happen to your house and possessions. Discos work particularly well in the sort of large space provided by a community center, church social hall or leisure center. They are not expensive to book.

Reserve both disco and hall well in advance as they can be much in demand, particularly at weekends. Make sure when you reserve that the disco has the kind of music your children want, especially if their tastes are at all out of the ordinary, then talk to the DJ in detail during the week before the party so as to make sure that he plays any favorites and to remind him of your requirements.

Barbecues are generally popular with teenagers, even more so if you can hold one on a beach, though you should check with the local government to see if this is against local laws or if permission is needed. Picnics are popular at the younger end of the age range.

If you are feeling really flush, then see if your local restaurant has a room for private parties and reserve a sit-down dinner. Adult behavior is definitely on the menu!

Make diagonal cuts 1 inch apart along the length of the French bread, cutting three quarters of the way through it. Cream together the butter, garlic, parsley, and add salt and pepper to taste. Spread the mixture liberally between the slices, and then spread any remaining butter over the top.

Wrap in foil and bake in the oven for 10 minutes. Draw the foil back to expose the top of the loaf, then cook for a further 5 to 10 minutes until crisp. Remove the foil and cut through each slice.

Pizza

SERVES 18

Dough
3 cups plain flour
1 teaspoon salt
1 teaspoon dried yeast
1 teaspoon sugar
1/2 pint warm water
2 tablespoons oil

Topping
3 tablespoons oil
3 large onions, chopped
3 × 14 oz cans tomatoes, drained
and chopped
2 teaspoons oregano
salt and pepper
3 tablespoons tomato purée
1 lb Mozzarella cheese,
thinly sliced
2 × 2 oz cans anchovy
fillets, drained and halved
18 black olives, halved and stoned

Sift the flour and salt into a bowl. Dissolve the yeast and sugar in a little of the water and leave in a warm place for 10 minutes. Add to the flour, together with the remaining water and the oil. Mix to a soft dough.

Turn on to a floured surface and knead for 10 minutes, until smooth and elastic. Place in a

clean bowl, cover and leave to rise in a warm place for about 1½ hours, until it has doubled in size.

Heat the oil in a pan, add the onions and fry until soft. Add the tomatoes and oregano, and season to taste; cook for 5 minutes.

Heat the oven to 450°F. Turn the dough on to a floured surface and knead it for a few minutes. Divide it into three equal pieces, roll each into 10 inch circle and place them on greased baking sheets. Spread 1 tablespoon

If the weather is right for going outdoors, a barbecue offers a way of making the meal interesting. Try to make the food portable – pitta bread makes a good vehicle, as with these spare ribs and sausages.

of tomato purée over each round. Divide the tomato mixture between the rounds and cover it with cheese. Arrange the anchovies and olives on top. Bake in the oven for 15 to 20 minutes until the dough edges are crisp.

FORMAL PARTIES

Whether grand setpieces for important celebrations or intimate evenings with friends, formal parties enable you to entertain on the Rolls Royce level.

The line between informal and formal parties is not a hard and fast one, but in broad terms the formal party requires a level of dressing up on the part of the guests, or incorporates a sitdown meal, or both. Whereas there are no rules for informal parties, various codes of etiquette come into play with formal ones.

Almost any party can be made formal: you can transform an ordinary evening party into something that resembles a gala night at the opera by specifying evening dress. However, if more is required of the guests than at a casual party, far more is required of the host and hostess. These are impressive occasions, and therefore one must impress. Beer is out, champagne or fine wines are in, with food of corresponding quality. At a large stand-up affair, hired waiters, not the host and hostess, carry the trays. Naturally, these occasions involve sizable expense.

But while only millionaires, businesses and ambassadors can afford regular evening-dress parties, there are formal occasions that come more easily within the means of most people, and which fit happily into a normal lifestyle. Usually these involve entertaining on a smaller scale. A dinner party for two other couples is in itself a semi-formal occasion.

But if a lot of work goes into formal parties, there can also be more satisfaction. A successful formal party is truly an event of which one can justly be proud.

A formal party calls for elegance and style, but can still also be a very relaxed and friendly occasion, even in a grand setting.

Dinner Parties

The dinner party is the most exposed form of entertaining. Essentially only a few people will be invited, so they have to be chosen with a view to a mix that creates flowing conversation. As the party is built around the meal, the food is the focus of attention, so this is the time to pull out the stops in the kitchen, prepare your best dishes, and present them in a careful, attractive way.

Every dinner party starts with the guests. "Who are we going to invite?" precedes "What are we going to eat?" For most of us, after the first impulse has registered of wanting to have people over for dinner, we begin by thinking of a particular couple we would like to invite.

Choosing the guests

If you have plenty of time, it can be a good idea to ask these people first, to establish that they can come, before building the rest of the guest list. But whether you do this or just take the chance, the search is then on for other people who will go well with them. Think first in terms of the total numbers. Twelve is usually the limit, both in terms of the space available and the range of matching china and cutlery, and also from the point of conviviality. Beyond twelve the feeling of a single event shared gets lost.

Feelings as to what is the "right" number depends very much on temperament and on the personalities invited, but it is worth bearing in mind that a single conversation can be carried on by six people, while eight break up predominantly into two or three conversations.

A slight taboo exists in some people's minds over inviting odd numbers of people. This should be challenged. There is nothing wrong with inviting two single people whom we think may get on together, provided that there is no attempt at matchmaking, which will only embarrass everybody concerned. But if you have a single friend you want to ask, you could in fact be doing

Odd numbers

Odd numbers of guests only create a problem with formal seating. Whereas for a very formal dinner party, in which the men come in their tuxedos, the rule of seating man-woman-man-woman holds good, with more casual affairs one can happily put people of the same sex next to each other. A good arrangement with the single "extra" man would be: man-man-woman-woman-man-man-woman, and *vice versa* for a spare woman. Under this arrangement everyone has a member of each sex to each side.

them and yourself a disfavor by inviting another single just to make up the numbers.

When choosing guests, think of those who have similar interests but different careers. If you concentrate on people who have the same kind of job as you, there is a danger of the evening being spent talking "shop", to the boredom of any other guest from a different walk of life.

When the guests arrive, bring in these interests when you introduce them to each other; it can be a great ice-breaker. This does not mean that you have to be brutally overt about it, but you can find a relaxed way of raising the subject.

Planning the menu

Dinner parties are meant to impress, so go for dishes that are high on style. On the other hand, prepare to compromise a little: you don't want to spend all your time in the kitchen and then arrive a frazzled wreck at the table.

Good presentation is essential. From the anchovy eggs through the fillet steak to the cheese and fruit the food in this meal is even further enhanced by the beautiful china, glass and cutlery.

The amount and timing of preparation provide the key. A cold appetizer or one that can be brought to the right temperature just before serving, followed by a main dish that can be left to itself while you enjoy the first course, avoids a lot of running around and having to think of several things at once.

Decide on the main course first, choosing a recipe that you have already mastered. This can be as lavish as you wish, but if you go for something simple, remember that it can be made to look more lavish with the help of some thoughtful garnishes.

The nature of the main dish determines the choice of appetizer. Avoid repeating elements: vol-au-vents followed by boeuf-en-croûte will have your guests quietly speculating on whether an apple pie is going to round off a trio of pastries. Watch particularly for hidden ingredients like cream that play a large part in determining the character of the dish in which they are included. Finally, think of consistency; soup followed by a casserole is fine only for those having trouble with their dentures!

If you are having a rich main course, then a simple appetizer like an avocado vinaigrette or some melon will leave appetites relatively unimpaired and palates awake. But if you decide on a simpler main course, you could put more of your culinary skill into starting the meal with an imposing flourish.

Desserts should not pose too much of a problem. There are many wonderful dishes that can be prepared in advance and left in

Cutlery is laid with the items to be used first on the outside.

Planning ahead

- Check whether your guests have any special dietary requirements.
- Make sure you have a clean tablecloth and napkins a couple of days in advance.
- Buy ingredients the day before, to allow for anything that might be unobtainable.
- Prepare as much in advance as possible.
- Decide what you are going to wear.

---

the refrigerator or freezer: ice creams, sherbets, layer cakes, fruit compôtes, cheesecakes, chiffon pies, mousses. A lot of hot dishes like pies, tarts and sweet soufflés can at least be prepared partly in advance and put in the oven to cook while you eat the main course.

As with appetizers, the choice of dessert is determined by the main course, with an eye on avoiding repetition and providing contrast. Many a guest who cannot manage the last mouthful of salmon or pheasant manages to

find room for a crème brûlée or apple sherbet, just because the change of flavor revives the flagging appetite.

Cheeses are sometimes put out with the drinks before the meal, but they can be offered, as is the normal custom in France, between the main course and the dessert. A selection of three or four is necessary to provide sufficient variety to appeal to everyone, with at least one soft cheese, one hard one and one blue one. Likewise a choice of different crackers provides that extra touch of thoughtfulness.

Ethnic cuisines
All these principles go out of the window if you want to serve one of the world's great non-European cuisines. With Indian food, apart from a little taster served with the pre-dinner drinks and some optional fruit at the end, all the dishes should be served together. By contrast, the Chinese serve their dishes one by one, leaving each on the table until it is finished, but as this means constant trips to the kitchen it is only on if you have a waiter.

NAPKIN ART

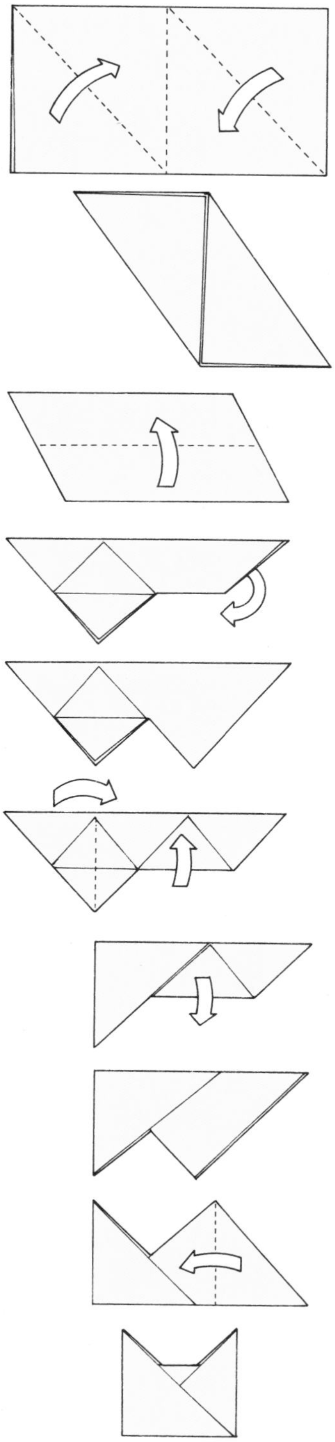

1

2

3

4

5

6

7

8

9

10

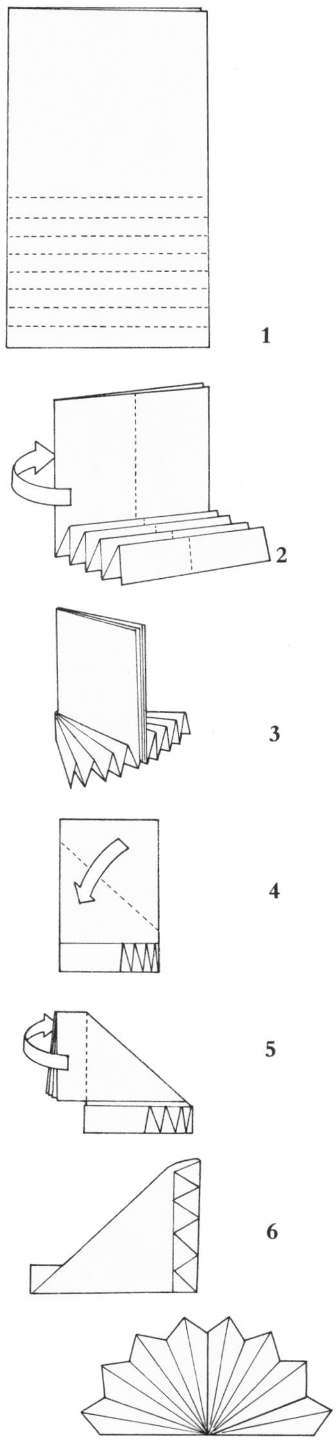

1

2

3

4

5

6

7

The Bishop's Mitre

1 Fold a square napkin in half, so that the edges are at the bottom. Find the center by folding it in half again. Crease and reopen. Bring the upper right-hand corner of the napkin down to bottom center and the lower left-hand corner up to top center.
2 Turn the napkin over and through 45 degrees.
3 Fold it in half again by bringing the bottom edge up to the top. This will leave the left-hand corner of the other side visible.
4 From beneath the right-hand side pull down the point of the napkin.
5 Lift up the right-hand point to the top edge.
6 Bring the left-hand end over to the edge of the triangle you have just made.
7 Pull down the napkin point on the right.
8 Holding the top edge with both hands, flip the napkin over.
9 Bring the right-hand point over the left, tucking it into the left-hand fold. Turn the napkin over and tuck the left-hand flap into the left-hand fold.
10 Stand the mitre up and open out its base so that it is free-standing. Carefully smooth out the folds.

The fan

(This shape is best made with a dressed cotton fabric, which will hold the fan folds firmly.)
1 Fold a square napkin vertically into two halves.
2 Starting at the bottom, fold upwards in accordion pleats about 1 inch deep until you have reached just past the half-way point.
3 Fold the pleated napkin in half vertically, with the pleats on the outside.
4 Fold down the top right-hand corner to the top of the pleats.
5 Fold the left-hand overlap back above the edge of the pleats.
6 Place the napkin on the table and let it unfold. The material just folded back will act as a support.
7 Check all the creases have been firmly pressed into the fabric.

Setting the table

It is said that presentation is half the secret of good cooking, and it is certainly true that a well prepared table gets the dinner off to a good start. Probably only the smell of burning from the kitchen is more off-putting than the sight of poorly washed cutlery and smeared glasses at the dinner table. When you lay the table, have a slightly dampened cloth to hand to give glasses and cutlery a final polish.

Unless you have a beautifully polished table that needs no cover, your best tablecloth and napkins should come out of the drawer. If you find that there is a stain in the tablecloth that you just have not been able to remove, say from red wine, cover it with a strategically placed serving mat. And if you simply do not not have enough matching napkins for the number of people, use equal numbers of two different ones, rather than having an odd couple amongst six all the same. Make a virtue of necessity and alternate them around the table. Alternatively use good-quality soft paper ones.

Set cutlery in the order it is to be used, starting at the outside. The exception is the dessert spoon and fork which are brought to the table later, with the dessert. The butter knife goes either on the extreme right of the last knife or on the side plate.

The same rule applies to wine glasses. If you are serving a different wine with each course, you will almost certainly be having white with the appetizer and red with the main course, so the white wine glass goes on the right, followed by the red, with a dessert wine glass to its left.

Folding the napkins on top of the side plate is all that is required of you, but if you want to be more elaborate there are various forms of napkin art you can follow. Practise well in advance as a collapsing Bishop's Mitre looks sloppy and doesn't inspire confidence in the food to follow.

If you are serving a cold appetizer, then it can be placed on the table in advance so that when your guests sit down it is ready to greet them. Whereas this is an impressive touch, do not do it if you are having your pre-dinner chat and aperitif in the same room as you are eating in, as it will create the suspicion that the dish is not quite fresh, especially if people have been smoking.

Seating guests

The guiding principle for formal parties is to alternate men and women (see p.44), though as soon as rigid formality is dropped it is not essential. For parties of six or ten, place the host and hostess at opposite ends of the table; for eight and 12, as nearly opposite as possible. For such occasions, put elegantly written place cards in the center of each setting, or above the space for the plate. If you are not doing this, invite people to sit according to a pre-arranged scheme; telling people to sit where they like might seem relaxed but in practice it only leads to confusion.

One way of getting everybody to mix is make them change places after each course.

Decorating the table

Flowers have a complementary role to play with food. They bring color and freshness to the table, and a reminder of the natural state from which the cooked food originated.

Dining table flowers should be of a scale and size to match the table, and never so tall that people have to crane their necks to see around them to the person opposite. They are meant to be noticed, but not to be so grand as to be an obstruction or distraction. On the other hand, a tiny bouquet can get lost on a large dinner table, but two or three of them at well-placed intervals will have a charming effect. Decide on whether you want the table to have a single focal point, or whether you want to break it up into different centers of attention.

Fresh flowers should be in peak condition. Your guests are going to be sitting in front of them for a couple of hours and are going to have plenty of time for wilting stems and fading blooms to come to their attention. Buy them on the day, or no more than one day before, and give the stems proper treatment as advised in flower-arranging manuals.

Fresh flowers are not, however, the only option. Beautifully made silk flowers are now widely sold, and can be arranged in advance, so

are one less thing to worry about on the day. The same applies to dried flowers, which have a prettily faded look. However, they are fragile, so only use them if they are not going to be in the way of cuffs and sleeves.

Table decorations must look good from every angle. Keep turning your arrangement around as you make it to ensure that it is attractive from all sides.

None of these strictures about size and all-round appearance apply to sideboard arrangements. Here you can indulge yourself with a tall or sweeping display, made to be admired from the front. Avoid highly scented flowers, though, as their perfume will fight with the flavor of the food.

Candlelight enhances any dinner table, casting a warm light

This display of carnations, chincheree, gypsophila, delphiniums and ferns shows how arrangements need lose nothing in grandeur just because they are low in height.

and bouncing little-pin-prick highlights off glasses and silver. It is worth investing the small bit extra in non-drip candles. But don't rely entirely on candles as they do not create enough light.

Pre-dinner drinks

Plan on sitting down to eat about 45 minutes after the time you have asked your guests to arrive. This allows latecomers a pardonable half hour and lets guests get to know each other over a drink before dinner.

Some gourmets swear that drinking spirits before a meal dulls the palate, and that the only appropriate pre-prandial is a glass of dry sherry. But most people prefer the old favorites – whiskey, gin or vodka – or increasingly white wine. If you can let guests choose from a well-stocked bar, be prepared with slices of lemon, mixers, and ice decanted into a bowl or in a bag in the refrigerator.

If you do not have such a range at your fingertips, then try to offer a choice of two drinks, preferably contrasting in character such as sherry and gin and tonic, or just wine.

Wine

The matter of serving wine with food has never been simple, but when relatively few Americans drank wine, even fewer worried about suitability. You could get by with knowing what the major French wine areas were, that German wines were sweet and that most Italian reds were fruity.

But now that more people are drinking wine with their meals, standards have gone up, and the selection is larger – including some first-rate domestic wines – and choosing a suitable wine can seeem a bit daunting. Fortunately, the choice need not be so difficult. Many wines are known by their grape varieties, and these grapes are themselves familiar from France. Cabernet Sauvignon and Merlot are the two grape varieties used in red Bordeaux, Pinot Noir in red Burgundy, Chardonnay in white Burgundies such as Chablis, and Sauvignon for the dry whites of Bordeaux. Riesling is widely used for sweet wines, although not invariably, unlike Muscat, which is almost always used for dessert wines. It is worth getting to know these terms as many of the newer wines using them represent excellent value.

Meat traditionally calls for red wine, and fish for white, though the rule is now much breached. It often helps to think instead of "depth": rich food needs a solid, well-bodied wine to complement it, whereas a white fish will struggle unequally through the strong taste of a vintage French red.

Matching food and wine is an art, not a science, and there are always new combinations to be discovered. It is best, anyway, not to be dogmatic, and to provide both red and white, to allow for individual preference.

If you do, though, decide to go the whole hog and serve different wines with different courses, two guidelines will help. The appetizer should be accompanied by a white wine, unless it is a very meaty dish, because white wine leaves taste-buds in a state to enjoy the red wine that follows, while the reverse is not true. Secondly, desserts are for sweet wines with sufficient substance to stand up to them, such as Sauternes or a wine from the Muscat grape.

Glasses and decanting

Wine glasses come in many different shapes and sizes, and most homes will only have one type available. If you do have choice, then a white wine glass should be the taller, thinner one, and the red will have a round, wide bowl to allow the scent of the wine to develop. As this smell is an important ingredient in the enjoyment of red wines, red wine glasses should only be filled up to about half way, to allow the warm air to work on the wine's surface.

Wine temperatures

At room temperature: vintage Bordeaux and Burgundies and other vintage wines made from the same grapes; Rhône reds.

Cool room temperature: non-vintage Bordeaux, Burgundies and similar wines; Italian and Spanish reds.

After one hour maximum in refrigerator: dry and medium-dry whites, rosé, genuine champagne.

After two hours in the refrigerator: sweet wines, other sparkling wines.

The temperature at which wine is served is important. White wine tastes flat and uninteresting, even downright soapy, when warm, whereas the variety of flavor of red wine is generally stifled if the wine is cold. However, this does not mean simply sticking the white wine in the refrigerator for a day in advance, as this will make it too cold, or treating the red as if it were a baby's bottle and standing it in near-boiling water. A couple of hours in a warm room for red and no more than two hours in the refrigerator for white are enough.

Vintage reds benefit from decanting just before serving. This is because the wine will have a sediment at the bottom which is easily stirred up and can get into the glasses. The bottle is poured very slowly and carefully into the decanter, with a lighted candle under its neck so that you can see

the sediment the second it reaches it. At that point stop decanting.

After dinner
As with aperitifs, fashions in after-dinner drinks change, and liqueurs like Drambuie, Chartreuse and Cointreau that once were only served straight from the bottle are now often served on the rocks. The choice is as broad as you want it to be; for example, malt whisky makes an excellent after-dinner drink. The only principle is that they are all strong and are served without mixers.

Liqueurs are often best enjoyed away from the table, in comfortable chairs where a sense of wellbeing can radiate out from the stomach. In Britain, however,

Vintage Bordeaux and port should be decanted slowly and carefully so as not to disturb their sediments. Decanting also allows the wine to warm up and its flavor to develop.

port is traditionally drunk at the table, partially because of the European habit of having coffee in the living room; unlike liqueurs port does not go well with it.

Luncheon Parties

Lunch is a quite different occasion from dinner. The presence of daylight itself creates its own mood, and the character of the party is influenced by the realization that much of the day is still to follow. Sunday dinner is an especially good time for families to get together.

Apart from business entertaining, which can be on a very grand scale, and some family celebrations, luncheons are generally more modest than dinner parties. Because lunch is inherently less formal than dinner, most people will opt for a buffet if they want to entertain a large number of guests, and keep the sit-down lunch for just one or two other couples.

Family entertaining
Guests with children will expect them to be included in the invitation, though it should be made clear at the time of asking. Finding baby-sitters in the middle of the day, when children are going to be very much awake and at their most active, is quite a different matter from getting someone around in the evening to sit quietly in front of your television. Moreover, most parents want to spend time with their children at the weekend, as there is not much space for family time during the week. So if you do not want to include children it may be best to reconsider your guest list or the time of day you are asking them over.

Young children may not care for the ham and chicken mousseline or the eggplant soufflé that you have lovingly prepared. They may also not be able to wait for them: childish appetites are very demanding and allow no room for the concept of waiting. It is therefore often advisable to prepare something different for them, and to serve it up in advance of the adult meal, particularly if you are expecting to have this on the late side. If you feel that this is excluding the children, then either organize the meal so that it is served in good time, or provide some light snacks to keep them going.

Food
The simplicity of a luncheon is reflected in the food. Two courses are quite adequate – which does not mean that you cannot provide an appetizer, but that it is fair to assume lunch appetites on average will be smaller than evening ones.

Lighter dishes are much in order – quiches, soufflés, salads,

Roast beef with Yorkshire puddings, roast potatoes, spring greens and leeks, rounded off with a fruit pie or an English trifle, make a perfect traditional Sunday lunch.

PIPING CREAM TO MAKE PATTERNS ON DESSERTS

1 Whisk cream until it forms peaks. Put in a piping bag with a small rosette nozzle.

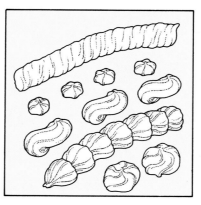

2 Hold the piping bag firmly and squeeze it gently in bursts to form your design.

fish, omelettes. Alternatively, exploit the fact that less show is expected of lunch, and that it is more of a family meal, to serve more home-style recipes such as stuffed jacket potatoes.

The exception to the principle of lightness is the traditional Sunday dinner, built around a roast, which is always popular, especially with children – beef, ham, chicken, loin of pork, or duck (you are quite likely to need two). But even though the food will be rich and filling, the emphasis is still on

A good selection of cheeses, served with a fine red wine, almost makes a meal in itself. From the top clockwise: *Caboc, Crédiou, goat's cheese, Camembert, Stilton, Cheddar with Walnuts, Brie, curd cheese in vine leaves, and* middle *roulé with herbs.*

simplicity, with good quality ingredients, simply cooked, being the keynote.

Buying fish

Always check that the fish is very fresh, which can be recognized from firm flesh, clear eyes, bright red gills and clean smell. Fish counters will offer to "clean" whole fish for you. If you would rather do it yourself, it involves slitting the belly and taking out the gut, snipping the gills with scissors, and washing it thoroughly.

Discard any shellfish that smell or look the slightest bit dubious, and any mussels that do not open in cooking.

Foods that are slow to digest might be all right on a Sunday, but it is best to steer clear of fried and heavy foods if any guests are going to work in the afternoon. Spicy dishes like chili are also best avoided as the taste can remain with people for the rest of the day.

What to drink

The time of week as well as the time of day is again a significant factor when planning what to drink. Dinner on a cold winter Sunday might lend itself to a strong wine and liqueurs afterwards. But if you are expecting to do anything more active in the afternoon than slumping in armchairs, then alcohol will have to be more muted. This does not mean that no thought has to go into the choice of wines; on the contrary, they must be as carefully considered as for an imposing dinner.

Lighter reds such as most non-vintage Californian, Oregon or New York state wines, regional

French, or carafe wines are suitable accompaniments to meat-based main courses.

Fish is a popular choice for lunch, so a dry white wine will be safe, although more meaty fish like salmon and tuna go perfectly well with red. Vegetarian dishes provide more of a problem; your first feeling might be that they should be accompanied by white wine, but white is sometimes too sharp for the vegetable or for the sauce it is served in. Egg- and cheese-dominated dishes go better with red wine.

Dessert wines are best omitted as, despite their sweetness, they are strong in alcohol.

Keep aperitifs to wine-based drinks such as sherry or vermouth. Except for the hardened drinker, heads in the middle of the day have less defense against the assault of hard liquor.

Have plenty of mineral water on the table, to help wash down the food.

Desserts

If you are serving only two courses, you may find that you have more time to pull out the stops on a dessert than you do in preparing a dinner party. Your best pie - lemon meringue, strawberry, pecan, whatever - will surely please your guests. Don't, however, serve a hot dessert after a cold main course, as this unbalances the meal. A good alternative would be a spectacular layer cake, or perhaps an angel food cake with the center filled with raspberries, chopped peaches or home-made fruit sherbert.

For an even more impresive finale do a Baked Alaska or a Bavarian cream. If your guests are fairly cosmopolitan, you might offer a European-style finish to

the meal, providing a cheese course followed by fresh fruit, especially if the main course is fairly light.

Make the cheeseboard look fresh with grapes, figs or other small fruit scattered around, and vine leaves or parsley sprigs. Top restaurants have no compunction about putting out cheeses that have done the rounds before, so there is no reason why yours should come straight from the delicatessen either. However, remove any bits of other cheeses or butter that have got on to them first.

Select the cheeses from the following popular choices:

BLUE CHEESES: Stilton, Blue Brie, Gorgonzola, Roquefort, Dolcelatte

SOFT CHEESES: Brie, Camembert, Port Salut

SEMI-HARD CHEESES: Edam, Gouda, Emmenthal, Gruyère, Bel Paese, Tomme au Raisin

HARD CHEESES: Cheddar, Montery Jack, Vermont, Colby, Grana

GOAT AND SHEEP CHEESES: Pecorino, Ricotta, chèvre (any French cheese made from goat's milk).

Italian-style lunch

Lunch is an important feature of the day in Mediterranean countries. Why not draw from the wonderful cuisines by giving a completely Italian meal? A typical menu would be: prosciutto ham with melon, followed by veal escalopes or pasta with a pesto sauce, both alternatives served with a green salad. Follow with a zabaglione, a sherbet or a zuppa inglese. Serve with a Valpolicella, Soave, Chianti or Orvieto.

Formal Buffets

A buffet provides the basis for a party when you want to invite more people for a meal than you can comfortably seat around a table. It provides a good oppportunity for the guests to mingle, and for more intimate conversation than is possible in the public arena of a dinner table. Buffets can also be served at any time of day, to late evening.

One of the great joys of a buffet party is that you do not have to worry so much about the compatability of the guests. With a dozen people around a dinner table you will have to consider whom to invite on the basis of their getting on and how best to seat them. At a buffet party the same number are going to move around and can find themselves whom they best get on with. However, this is not an excuse for irresponsibility in drawing up the guest list; any number of people looking glum because none of them really get along is no party for anyone!

Preparation
A buffet party is not a cocktail party, and although people will be standing when they help themselves to food, for much of the time they are going to be sitting down. You therefore need to set out chairs in advance in

A buffet meal can be presented with as much panache and extravagance as a sit-down dinner. From bottom left: croquettes of fish, stuffed eggs, tomato mayonnaise, chicken and ham vinaigrette, herb bread, fricadelles, apple flan, farmhouse cheese and ginger cake.

small groups, and to include a small table with each group. The point of this is not to provide a surface to eat from – the food should be manageable with the plate perched on the lap or held in one hand – but somewhere for empty plates, glasses and ashtrays. Include dining chairs, since deep armchairs and sofas are not the easiest of places from which to eat. Clear spaces as well on mantelpieces and shelves for the empty plates and glasses. Otherwise they will end up on the floor, where one or more will eventually get stepped on.

In general, buffets need a lot of preparation, with the room to get ready, a large number of dishes to cook, and much of the work of dividing them into portions that is normally done at the table done in advance. On the other hand, there is the great advantage that it can all be done in advance, leaving you free to mingle and to enjoy yourself.

Presentation
Good presentation is important to any entertaining, and the buffet is no exception. Only your best serving dishes, china and cutlery will do, as anything less looks too casual. Have all the plates,

napkins and knives and forks set out before people arrive, and display them neatly and attractively. Liven the table up with special food-related decorations and with flowers.

If the party is large it may not be possible to put all the forks together and all the knives together without producing an unacceptable heap. In such cases make groups of a dozen or so each, and put them at opposite ends of the table. With large numbers it is best to divide all the food up into two, and have each complete set on a separate table, or at different ends of the same table. Otherwise you will have a long line of hungry people trying not to look as impatient as they feel.

Always put the plates where the guests will come to them first, followed by the main ingredients of the course, and then the side dishes. There are distinct pros and cons about whether you put out the desserts with the main course. If you do, then everyone will know what is to follow before risking overfilling themselves with the main course, and you allow people to eat at their own pace. You also don't have to worry any more about getting food from the kitchen and you can get on with enjoying yourself. On the other hand, the desserts will not be at their freshest when they make it on to individual plates, and could get in the way of the main course. The amounts of food and the limited space available might decide the issue for you.

If you have the option, serve the food in another room from the one where the guests are congregating. This enables you to put the food out in advance, and to announce the eating time with a flourish.

The appearance of the food is as important as the display of the implements for eating it. Decorate cold plates with parsley sprigs and elaborate garnishes such as tomato roses, radish waterlilies or green onion tassels.

The food

You are going to need knives, if only because spreading butter on to a bread roll with a finger tip is more than a little messy! But

Preparing the food in advance

- carve meat into small slices
- cut quiches into portions
- portion salmon and remove from the bone without destroying its shape
- slice all bread
- shred and chop lettuce
- slice hard-boiled eggs
- cut pastry-based desserts and cakes into portions

buffet food should all be served in a way that it can be eaten single-handed. The word "buffet" has two "f"s in the middle – for finger food and fork food!

Finger food means canapés, open-face sandwiches, vol-au-vents, and things like spicy shrimps or deep-fried mushrooms that can be served on toothpicks.

Fork food is not necessarily sloppy – meats, fish and quiches are the foundation of many an excellent buffet, but they have to be sliced and cut into mouth-sized pieces in advance. With

quiches, separate the portions with a small garnish such as slices of tomato or parsley sprigs.

Deep-fried mushrooms

SERVES 10

2lbs button mushrooms
oil for deep frying
Batter
2 cups all-purpose flour
pinch of salt
2 tablespoons oil
1¼ cups water
4 egg whites

First make the batter. Sift the flour and salt into a bowl, then gradually beat in the oil and water. Whisk the egg whites until stiff, then fold into the batter.

Drop the mushrooms into the batter. Heat the oil in a deep-fryer to 375°F. Deep-fry the mushrooms in batches, lifting them from the batter to the oil, using a slotted spoon. Drain them on paper towels and keep them hot while frying the rest.

Serve with a garlic mayonnaise.

A TOMATO ROSE FOR THE BUFFET TABLE

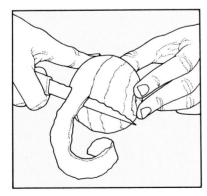

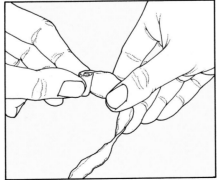

1 Starting at the smooth end of a tomato, cut a continuous strip of skin ½ inch wide. Use a firm tomato only.

2 With the flesh inside, curl from the base end, forming a bud shape between the fingers.

3 Continue winding the strip of skin around the bud and it will make the form of a rose. Place carefully on a plate.

Quiche paysanne

MAKES 16 SMALL PORTIONS

³/₄ cup all-purpose flour, sifted
³/₄ cup wholewheat flour
5 tablespoons margarine
4–5 tablespoons iced water

Filling

1 tablespoon butter
1 tablespoon oil
4 slices bacon, chopped
1 large onion, chopped
2 potatoes, sliced
2 eggs
1¹/₂ cups heavy cream
1 tablespoon each chopped parsley
and chives
³/₄ cup Cheddar cheese, grated

Place the flours and salt in a bowl and rub in the margarine until the mixture resembles fine breadcrumbs. Add enough water to make a firm dough. Turn on to a floured surface and knead lightly. Roll out the pastry and use it to line a 9 inch quiche pan. Prick the pastry all over and chill for 30 minutes. Heat the oven to 375°F.

Line the pastry with foil weighed down with dried beans and bake blind in the preheated oven for 12–15 minutes, until set. Remove the foil and beans and return to the oven for a further 5 minutes.

Heat the butter and oil in a pan, add the bacon and cook until

A buffet is a good way of entertaining large numbers to a meal, particularly for special celebrations such as weddings. Seating is often limited, and finger food is best.

lightly browned. Drain on paper towels. Add the onion and potatoes to the pan and cook for 12 to 15 minutes, until browned. Drain on kitchen paper.

Beat the eggs and cream together, stir in the herbs and season well with salt and pepper. Spoon the potatoes, onion and bacon into the pastry shell. Pour over the egg mixture and sprinkle with the cheese. Return to the oven for 20 to 25 minutes, until well risen and golden brown.

Weddings

Any house with enough room to take a party is large enough for a wedding reception, and home is an especially fine place to entertain people for this unique combination of personal, family and public celebration.

As it is only a very large home that will have room for 40 or 50 people to sit down to a wedding breakfast, your reception is most likely to be a buffet, and much of the advice given on pages 56–9 applies here. However, because there are so many other things to think about on the wedding day, as much as possible has to be done in advance. The last thing you want to fill your mind during the ceremony is worries about unmade salads and warm champagne.

Of course, you can get in professional caterers. Reserve them well in advance and be prepared to discuss your requirements with them at least a couple of weeks before the wedding. As they will be experienced in this kind of function, they will have plenty of suggestions of suitable food and drink to serve, and appropriate quantities, all at a range of prices. Having agreed on everything, you should be able just to vacate your kitchen for them on the morning of the wedding, and then let them get on with it.

Getting help
If you decide to do all the catering and organizing yourself, it is still essential to get some help, and should not be difficult to find someone by asking around.

During the reception there is a continuous flow of dishes and glasses in and out of the kitchen, and constant cleaning up to be done. The host and hostess should not be struggling to function as waiters, but should be looking after the guests from the moment they shake the first hand until well after the happy couple's car has clattered off down the road with its train of empty cans.

Don't underestimate the work involved in cleaning up afterwards. You will not be feeling at your most energetic then, and the help of other people will disperse some of the "flat" feeling that usually follows.

To mark such an important event good-quality cutlery and plates are essential, as are good linen (preferably damask) or cotton tablecloths for the tables and proper glasses for the champagne. Borrow or rent what you lack yourself. Catering services can usually provide them, and some laundries will supply tablecloths.

Flowers
Flowers are almost as important in the reception as they are in the ceremony. A large display on a pedestal in the hall is particularly welcoming. There is no need to stick to the pinks, yellows and whites normally associated with

wedding flowers. The chances are that these colors will have dominated the bouquet, but you can greet the guests with bright, bold color combinations.

Put smaller arrangements out on the tables, certainly on the buffet table itself, and smaller arrangements on any side tables. You do not have to stick to traditional-style arrangements:

Reception countdown

Three to four weeks ahead: Order the wedding cake, unless making it yourself.

Two weeks ahead: Reserve all equipment to be rented.

One week ahead: Make quiches and any other dishes that will freeze. Order all food. Collect champagne, wine and other drinks.

Two days ahead: Make salad dressings, cook all meat, fish and vegetables that are to be served cold. Make cake, if making it yourself.

The day before: Prepare salads, prepare or cook desserts, pâtés and terrines. Prepare hot food as far as can be done. Position and set the table. Prepare the rooms.

Early on the day: Put out all food on serving dishes, add whipped cream to desserts, dress salads, make canapés, cook hot foods and leave warming, chill champagne.

garlands looped along a long table can look stunning, or if you are adventurous try scattering petals on the table top.

Toasting the couple

Champagne, or at least a very good sparkling wine, is, of course, essential to toast the various parties at the end of each speech. Apart from expense, there is no reason why it should not be served throughout the reception, but as an alternative provide a good, dry white wine while people are eating. Another common practice is to give people an aperitif when they arrive, but whatever you go for make sure that guests are handed a drink as soon as they have been officially received.

Expect a good turnout of children, so provide adequate supplies of fruit juices and carbonated beverages, allowing some for adults too.

After the bride and groom have made their exit the reception starts to wind down, so it is a good point to offer coffee. Have the ingredients prepared so that you are not having to grind mountains of beans.

Speeches are the prelude to toasts.

Food

Cold food for the main course is usually the order of the day, if only because of the problems of serving large amounts of hot food at a buffet. If you do not have a helper to stand by the table and carve as people turn up, preslice cold roast beef, pork or ham, or whole chickens or turkey, but do leave the joint out on the table with some meat still on it. Somehow it looks a bit stingy just to leave slices, as if you are rationing what people eat.

Instead of serving the cold meats "neat" you can go for interesting variations, such as mildly curried chicken or a galantine of turkey and veal.

Whole salmon is a perennial favorite, served with home-made mayonnaise, or fish baked in a pastry dish as in a koulibiac. Make sure that there is something, too, for vegetarians such as cheese and onion quiche. Set it on one side so that it isn't consumed by the carnivores.

Provide a good selection of salads so that there are enough for people to be able to make a choice:

potato salad, green been vinaigrette, tomato and onion, green salads, and salads with cold pasta, rice or other grains.

Desserts are going to be overshadowed by the cake, so for that reason most people do not serve any dessert other than ice cream. If you do decide to serve them, avoid pies and tarts, especially if you have served up pastry in finger foods or in the main course. Fresh fruit of the season with cream or a fruit compôte will round off the meal while leaving room for what is to follow.

CUTTING A ROUND CAKE

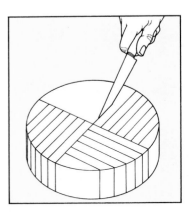

Cut first into four, then cut sections from each quarter.

PIPING ROSES FOR CELEBRATION CAKES

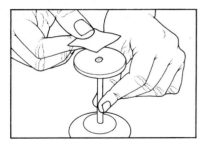

1 Half-fill an icing bag with stiff royal icing. Secure a square of paper to the icing nail with a dab of icing.

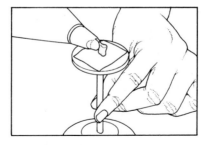

2 With thin end of petal nozzle uppermost, squeeze bag evenly while twisting nail, to pipe coil for rose center.

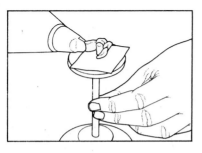

3 Add petals, by piping the icing in a single squeeze for each and twisting the nail. Take each petal about three-quarters the way around flower.

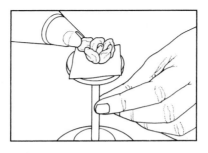

4 Pipe 4–6 petals, keeping the base towards the center each time. Leave to dry for 24 hours before removing paper.

The cake

The *pièce de resistance* is naturally the cake. By the time the wedding day dawns all that should be left is to cut it. Both cake and filling are pretty well hallowed by time: a simple white cake with a fairly firm white icing, though chocoholics have been known to have a chocolate cake.

However, there is still considerable room for personalization. The cake could be hexagonal or octagonal instead of round or square, and the tiers can be separated from each other by pillars, European-style. But the main variation comes in the icing, and here for the cake-decorating enthusiast, all her art comes to the fore, with hearts, roses, butterflies, leaves, fans or stars, and borders in lacework, loops, ribbons or shells.

It is a once-in-a-lifetime occasion, and the cake will be photographed like a film star, so give it your very best!

A traditional tiered wedding cake without pillars, decorated with a cascade of icing roses.

CHILDREN'S PARTIES

Almost all parents will embark on giving a children's party at some time – and if you've got more than one child you could be giving two or three parties every year if you like to give one to celebrate each birthday. And yet they can be occasions that parents dread as they contemplate opening their homes to 20 toddlers or a dozen rowdy pre-teens. But the secret to giving successful children's parties, as always, is to plan well in advance.

Because of the different requirements and expectations of children as they grow from toddlers to teens, there is scope for endless variation in children's party-giving. In practice, however, there are three ingredients to successful children's parties – plenty to do, plenty to eat, and plenty of help.

Parents worry about giving children's parties because they feel that lots of children together in one place will be too difficult to control, that the house will get wrecked, that someone is bound to be sick – or cry – or fall over. But actually giving a children's party can be very enjoyable for adults as well as children so long as you approach it positively – yes, you need energy, but remember most parties only last two hours and so long as there's plenty of activity the time passes very quickly. And children come expecting to enjoy themselves, so you can build on this basic good will.

Lots of color, noise and activity are sure signs of a successful children's party.

Preparation

Any party requires preparation, and a children's party especially so, because not only do you have to provide food, drink and a pleasant setting, you also have to cater to the needs of youngsters whose values and expectations are very different from your own.

What kind of party?
The first thing to plan is what kind of party you are giving. This depends very much on the age of the children, the occasion you are celebrating and the time of year. Ideas for different age groups are given in the following pages, but there are a few general rules.

Most children's parties are to celebrate birthdays – this is the most important anniversary for any child and they continue to want a special celebration well into their teens. But there are other occasions too, such as religious festivals like Christmas, Passover or Easter, or secular holidays like the Fourth of July, Halloween or Thanksgiving which you might want to mark in a special way for the children.

The time of year is very important because it is undoubtedly easier if you can get the children out of doors to play energetic games or activities, especially once they are over four. Although it is very nice to give an outdoor party for toddlers, do bear in mind that your back yard must be safe and secure. Equally, if you're frightened for the safety of your prize geraniums you may feel more comfortable keeping the party inside or even away from the house altogether. However if you're giving a winter party, you need to plan a bit more carefully how to keep them amused indoors.

Obviously you are going to have to suit the party to the expectations and abilities of the different age groups. But whatever their age, keep it simple. If your theme is too elaborate or your games too complicated, you'll soon lose the attention of at least some of the group, and that's when things can get out of hand.

At home...
When you decide to give a party for your children, have a look at the space available in your home before you send out the invitations. If you really feel you only want to use one room, and it isn't very big, limit the numbers to ten or so. This can be difficult if your son or daughter wants to invite the whole class, but you have to be selective and most children understand this. If you've got plenty of room, obviously invite more, and if you have a garden big enough to play games in this is good too. Of course, toddlers don't take up very much room, but remember that they will probably be accompanied by adults at least until they are four, and these have to be accommodated too. In any case, it is essential at this age to have extra adults to help, to encourage shy children, calm down the over-wrought and especially to be ready to join excursions to the bathroom!

When you have decided which room is to be used, clear as much furniture out of it as possible, and especially remove or put well out of reach any breakables. If possible arrange to have the party food eaten in a different room so that it can all be set out earlier out of temptation's way.

...or away
If you really don't think you've got room or can't bear the thought of cleaning up afterwards, you could consider having the party somewhere else altogether. An ideal solution is to rent a local hall for the afternoon, somewhere with kitchen facilities for a meal and with plenty of room for running around. Or you can organize a trip to the park for a picnic in the summer, or to a swimming pool or gym. Many community centers now cater especially for children's parties, and you can rent the facilities and have a party meal provided for you on the premises. Alternatively, you can just arrange the activities and bring the children home for a meal afterward.

The time of day

Most birthday parties are given in the afternoon, which may mean after school if you want to give it on the actual day. There's something to be said for the "after school" party, because if you're at home you can prepare the house during the day without the children under your feet and getting over-excited and possibly overwrought with anticipation. However, younger children may be quite tired at this time of day after school and may not enjoy it as much as they might. Weekend parties or parties during the school vacation can be just as much fun if you have them in the morning or at lunchtime. Lunchtime is a good time for pre-school children too, if they don't go to afternoon kindergarten or nursery school. This is a good plan if there are older brothers or sisters at school, as the younger child can have a special time for his or her own little friends.

Once your children reach double figures, they start wanting to be treated in a more grown-up way. You can satisfy this on a

Food should be fun; pizzas can sprout faces and a cucumber be a caterpillar.

special occasion by allowing evening parties, starting at perhaps 6.30 or 7.00 pm. Always put a clear finishing time on the invitation.

A lot of people like to provide a going home gift at children's parties. However, this can become something of a tyranny, as children begin to expect – indeed demand – party bags stuffed with gifts and candies, which can become unnecessarily expensive.

It is perfectly all right just to offer a balloon and an inexpensive memento plus a piece of cake suitably wrapped – if it's a theme party the gift could be linked to the theme.

Getting help

Whatever kind of party you decide to hold for your children, always make sure you have plenty of help. This could simply be grandparents coming to help with the dishes, wiping faces and showing children where the bathroom is. Or it could be professional help in the form of an entertainer, a mobile disco with visiting DJ – or, if you really want a relaxing time – actually engaging one of the many companies who will take over the whole thing and run your children's party for you, with games, decorations, food, entertainment - and they do the dishes afterward!

If you are going to book someone to come and help in any of the above ways, make sure you know exactly what you are paying for, and if possible get a personal recommendation from someone else, or take up references. It can be very disappointing if you hire an inflatable for your back yard, pay your deposit in advance and then find that nothing turns up on the day. Make sure you're covered by insurance (theirs or yours) and always book well ahead. If the entertainer is a good one he or she will be booked up well in advance.

Whatever you decide, involve your children in the decision making, within reason. Everyone will be a lot happier if they know exactly what's happening, and if it's what they want, you'll all enter into the spirit of the thing – which is, of course, means having a really enjoyable party.

Party food

A party meal is central to children's parties but, as you can see from the above, it doesn't necessarily have to be in the afternoon, and indeed, even if it is, there are lots of delicious things you can serve apart from the conventional sandwiches, ice cream and cake.

Children's party food can be both fun to look at, tasty and nourishing. The secret is to have plenty of variety, to suit all tastes and tempt the most finicky eater. Ice cream and cake are essential, especially at a birthday party; but it is a good idea to give the refreshments a little balance, in the form of sandwiches and perhaps also a molded gelatin fruit salad. Let your imagination rip with different colors and decorations

Presentation is important. Make the food look fun as well as decorating the house to give it a festive air. Decorate the table with streamers, bright napkins and a fun tablecloth (use paper or plastic for ease of cleaning up). Cut sandwiches into shapes with pastry cutters.

If it's a birthday, then there has to be a cake, but lots of other festivals can be celebrated with a special cake too, such as a fruit cake (not too rich as children tend not to like it) with frosting for Christmas, or a dark chocolate cake with orange icing for Halloween. Most children prefer a simple iced white or chocolate cake. Even the more grown-up pre-teens enjoy a cake in a more interesting shape such as a horse and carriage or a baseball field. Or it's a good idea to make one in the shape of the age of your child. You can get one professionally made but it's much more satisfying to make one yourself.

Simple sponge base

2 cups cake flour
2 teaspoons baking powder
1 cup butter
1 cup sugar
4 medium eggs
a little milk, if necessary

Pre-heat the oven to 350°F. Put all these ingredients into a food processor or blender and mix thoroughly. The finished mixture should be firm but not too stiff (add a little milk if necessary). Grease and line a cake pan and bake for about 45 minutes until the cake is lightly browned and springy, and at such time as a

One way to make the food look special is to give it a theme. This prehistoric spread has "dinosaur" ribs, fruit spears and chocolate "rocks".

skewer inserted into the center comes out clean.

For a colored sponge, add cocoa powder to the dry ingredients or drops of food coloring to the mixture.

■ **Note** Avoid yellow food coloring that contains tartrazine.

Butter icing

1 lb confectioners' sugar
1 cup softened unsalted butter
lemon juice
a little milk, if necessary

Beat the butter with a wooden spoon until it is creamy in texture, then beat in the confectioners' sugar. Add a few drops of lemon juice to sharpen the taste.

This mixture will be very stiff, just right for building and modeling, but if you want to spread it over, thin it a very little with milk. Color with food coloring as required.

Glacé icing

1 lb confectioners' sugar
about 4 teaspoons warm water
and/or lemon juice

Sieve the sugar into a bowl; this is really important as it makes it easier and quicker to work. Add the water a drop at a time, drawing the sugar in from the sides of the bowl with a fork, or use a food processor or blender. The icing should coat the back of a spoon without dripping quickly. Beat well. Add flavoring and coloring as required.

> ### Edible accessories for novelty cakes
>
> - chocolate chips for tiles, eyes, buttons, etc.
> - licorice laces for whiskers, tails, edging
> - licorice candies for windows, knobs, wheels
> - squares of chocolate for windows, keys, chimneys, etc.
> - angelica for leaves
> - coconut for snowflakes or with green food coloring for grass
> - marzipan can be shaped into animals, flowers and people
> - M&Ms, gum drops or colored candies for roof tiles, paths, footballs, flower centers, or simply picking out names or numbers
> - ice cream wafers for roof tiles, fans etc. (depending on shape)

To make a shaped cake

1. Work out a simple design on a piece of tracing paper and draw the outline on to it. There are lots of cake decorating books available with templates which you can trace. Depending on your design, you will need either a rectangular pan about 11 × 9 inches, a round pan with a 9 inch diameter, a square pan 10 × 10 inch, or a loaf pan. Alternatively, you could use a shaped baking pan – these are available at large kitchenware departments, and can sometimes be rented from them.

2. Two days before the party, make a simple sponge base to the required shape for your design.

3. Turn out the cake and allow to cool, then lay it on a board base covered with aluminum foil. Cut the shape you want with a sharp pointed knife. Don't throw away the cuttings – you might well need them for chimneys, wheels, doors etc, which can be "cemented" into place with spare icing.

4. When cool, ice the basic shape with a thin layer of glacé icing and allow to set for at least two hours, or preferably overnight. Glacé icing gives a good smooth basis for icing a particular design, but if you are in a hurry you can use butter icing as the base layer, applying it thickly and smoothing it out with a palette knife. It tends to give a more textured base, but this can be disguised if necessary with the piped design over the top.

5. The day before the party give yourself plenty of time and space to apply the design. Use butter icing and a set of piping tools. Be careful when mixing food coloring – it's awfully easy to use too much so add only a few tiny drops at a time until you get the required color. Piping can give you most of the effects you need but there are also useful edible accessories which are quick to use and add variety. Once the cake is iced leave in a cool place until needed.

NUMERAL CAKES

Making numerals involves baking one or two cakes to the right size and cutting them to shape as shown. Parts that have to be stuck together should be joined with jam or butter cream.

One – 6 inch square sandwich cake, cut in half and stuck together. Two, Five, Six, Seven and Nine – one $11\frac{1}{2} \times 8\frac{1}{2} \times 1\frac{1}{2}$ inch slab cake. Three and Eight – two 8 inch round sandwich cakes cut and stuck together. Four – 7–10 inch square sandwich cake.

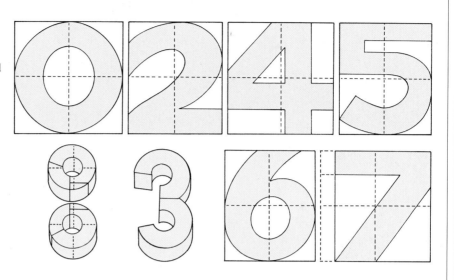

Toddlers

In some ways, giving a party for a group of toddlers is among the most rewarding of experiences. Children of this age are very easy to please and don't have the street-wise cynicism of some slightly older junior party-goers. And very often they'll be accompanied by one of their parents, so there'll be lots of extra people on hand to help.

You'll probably find that you give your first real children's party as parents when your first child is two. Of course, there's no real lowest age limit for baby parties, but even if you decide to give a party for your one-year-old, in effect you'll be having a pleasant get-together with a group of parents who have similar aged babies.

A two-year-old's party is different. Now you can begin to bring in some of the traditional ingredients of the children's party – with simple games and activities, and a delicious child-centered meal. Of course, much depends on the personality and development of your child. Some two-year-olds are gregarious and outgoing, others are shy and contrary, and all are unpredictable in their reactions to new situations. Much of what follows applies equally to three- to five-year-olds.

Planning a toddler party
Keep the guest list short, and never invite more than about ten. Young children (especially the host or hostess!) can become overwrought at parties but this is less likely if they are part of a small, intimate group of children they are reasonably familiar with.

Your first idea will probably be to think of giving the party in the afternoon, especially if it's a birthday celebration. But think carefully – this might not be convenient for parents with other children at school, so why not have your party in the morning and provide an early lunch? The food can be basically the same whatever time you choose.

If you have the party during the week, you may find that one or two of the toddlers are accompanied by babysitters, or grandparents if both parents work during the day. Weekend parties may make your adult head-count double if both parents come. If you definitely don't want older brothers and sisters there, choose a lunchtime or weekend for the party so you know there's someone else around to care for the older children.

Unless you know the children very well yourself – and they are comfortable in your home because they have visited many times before – it is worth making it clear that you would prefer under-threes to be accompanied by an adult anyway. So you have got to provide for their needs to an extent too, although a pot of coffee is quite acceptable.

Don't make the party too long.

An hour and a half is quite long enough for three years and under, and no more than two hours for the three-to-fives.

Even if you have had acceptances from everybody, it's a good idea to double-check on the morning of the party that everyone is still coming, as at this age colds and tummy upsets can strike suddenly.

Making the house safe
Toddlers are a joy to entertain, because they are so curious. The flipside of this is that you have to decide which parts of your home are going to be out of bounds for the party. If you have stairs that you don't want the children to climb, keep a safety gate in place at the bottom. Then put all your breakables or other precious items either out of reach or shut away in another room. Also move occasional tables or tables with sharp corners well out of the way so that the children can't bump their heads if they tumble over – and you can be sure that some of them will.

Ordinary sandwiches become something quite different when creatively arranged, as in this "house", served with meringue white mice, marshmallow tarts and cheese twigs.

Favorite snacks

- tiny cocktail sausages
- cubes of Cheddar or Swiss cheese
- tiny sandwiches, cut into shapes using novelty pastry cutters
- crackers spread with pâté or tangy cheese spreads
- celery chunks filled with cream cheese or with cottage cheese
- slices of cucumber, tomato, raw carrot, or other vegetables

Preparing the food

As with all children's parties, lay out the food in a different room from the main party area. It's preferable to have the meal somewhere like the recreation room which has an easy-to-clean floor, but if you're going to have it in a carpeted room put a large plastic sheet or old dust sheet under the table and chairs to save your carpet and your nerves from the onslaught. (You may also save a friend from the embarrassment of being parent to the one child that spills grapejuice on to the pale, delicately patterned woollen carpet that you're showing off for the first time.)

Most adult tables and chairs are too high for toddlers to sit at comfortably, so consider hiring small tables and chairs from a nursery school or kindergarten. Failing that, sit the children down on the floor on rugs and cushions around disposable or plastic table cloths laid out with food.

Don't provide paper or disposable plastic cups for under threes, as they are light and unstable. Instead, have a supply of sturdy plastic beakers and feeder cups for the youngest children.

Some dos and don'ts

Keep toddlers' food small and simple: Provide plenty of variety but don't overdo the quantities. Never use toothpicks – they can pierce the mouths or throats of unsuspecting young children. Peanuts, too, are a danger for children under five, for if a child chokes on a peanut it can set off a toxic reaction in the lining of the lung, so don't serve them. Some parents prefer their children not to have carbonated drinks, so it best to avoid them altogether for parties at this age. Cold chocolate milk is a great favorite. Finally, have a few warm damp face cloths handy to deal instantly with the inevitable sticky hands and faces.

Entertaining toddlers

Some people bring in a professional entertainer even for the youngest children, but this is neither necessary nor desirable. You'll have plenty of help anyway and some very young children find even the simplest entertainer daunting, if not downright frightening. However, this is not to say that even the littlest children aren't happy to join in simple games and songs.

Games for the under-threes

You'll find that some of games become hardy perennials, remaining popular even with occasional six-year-olds through their friendly familiarity! You may need some adult help but that all adds to the fun.

At this age games shouldn't be competitive; children just enjoy joining in. So if you want to do Musical Chairs, which many small children love, expect several to carry on even though they've been judged "out" several times! It is worth having one or two trial

Favorite sweets

Most children notoriously have a sweet tooth, and this is is particularly the case with toddlers. A party is not the time to be strict about limiting their indulgence of this, though not all the most popular foods have to be horrendously sticky. The following gives a good selection, bearing in mind there will also be a cake:
- marshmallows
- simple iced cookies
- little bowls of raisins
- ice cream - provide a choice of three provenly popular flavors
- chocolate cookies, brownies and cupcakes

rounds of each game so as to make sure that every child has got the idea. Although some of them will know the games already, there are bound to be some children who do not.

Ring-a-Ring o' Roses

Everyone holds hands in a circle and dances round singing this popular nursery rhyme. Naturally everyone falls down when commanded, and jumps up in the second verse. During the second verse, keep crouching down and just swing your hands backward and forward.

Ring-a-ring o' roses
A pocket full of posies
Tisha! Tisha!
We all fall down!

Picking up the daisies!
Picking up the daisies!
Tisha! Tisha!
We all jump up!

Pass the Parcel

This is a popular game in England, but it can travel.

Prepare a decent-sized parcel loosely wrapped with waste paper or colored tissue paper. Have more layers than children as at least one savvy two-year-old is bound to undo more than his fair share! Put a tiny treat in each layer, such as a chocolate chip.

Insert a suitable children's cassette, preferably with uninterrupted music, in a cassette player with a pause button. The children sit in a circle and pass the parcel around as the music plays. Then stop the music, and the person holding the parcel takes off a layer of paper.

Make sure the person operating the cassette player sees that every toddler gets a turn. When they get to the final layer, it's best not to have a big prize in the middle, but just another chocolate kiss or whatever, as younger children will find it hard to understand why everyone hasn't got a toy car or a box of crayons!

Musical Bumps

Using the same cassette, ask the children to dance around until the music stops, when they have to sit down and keep still. Last one down is out. Even some two-year-olds are surprisingly good at this game. It's a great appetite

Even at parties a lot of toddlers' activity is still individual.

rouser, so play it just before the meal then everyone will be happy to sit down for a rest!

Finger Play

For quiet moments when you want the children to sit down (for instance, straight after a big meal) simple finger games always hit the spot. Sit down at their level in front of them so they can copy you.

For the youngest children, try Peter and Paul. Everyone holds up their forefingers, deciding which is Peter and which is Paul. You then recite the words below and hide Peter and Paul alternately behind your back. The children will copy you slavishly!

Two little dickie birds
Sitting on a wall
One named Peter
One named Paul.
Fly away Peter
Fly away Paul.
Come back Peter
Come back Paul.

One of the most popular of these games is "The Eensy Weensy Spider". The words are as follows:

The eensy weensy spider
Went up the water spout.
Down came the rain
And washed the spider out.
Out came the sun
And dried up all the rain.
Eensy weensy spider
Went up the spout again.

On the first and last lines everyone rotates their thumbs and forefingers in a climbing motion.

On the second line both hands wave downward for rain, and then push sideways. The sun is represented by arching both hands over the head, and drying up the rain by a scooping movement.

Outdoor activities
Games can be played outside if you're having a fine weather party, but remember that some small children don't really like strong sun and may well prefer to sit in the shade. A simple outdoor game for under-threes is to let them chase soap bubbles around

Ideas for dressing up

The following all make popular themes for dressing up at parties:
- hats and masks
- face paints (make it a party activity)
- pirates
- cowboys and Indians
- circus characters
- animals or insects

the yard, trying to catch them or to burst them.

Three- to five-year-olds

You can begin to introduce more interesting games to your children's parties once they are over three. They particularly like to dress up, and at this age there is none of the embarrassment common among older children.

You could either make dressing up part of the fun by providing a huge box of suitable old clothes and hats, or suggest a theme for dressing up on the invitation. Don't make it too elaborate, because while some parents may be very creative or be sufficiently well off to rent a costume, others may be neither! Make it clear with a quiet word that your child's costume is going to be simple and home-made so that everyone else knows where they are. It isn't a competition – it's a way for the children to have fun, and at this age they are refreshingly unjudgmental.

The golden age for parties

In many ways, three to five is the golden age for children's parties. Children of this age seem to enter into the spirit of things and they really enjoy taking part. Because

Older pre-school children love any opportunity to dress up.

they don't mind being organized into groups and are more amenable to playing together, you can safely ask more than ten children, so long as you've got plenty of room, and a good adult support group.

There is scope for more complicated games at this age, such as games of tag if you've got a yard, or blindfold games for indoor parties. However, if you do have blindfold games like Blind Man's Buff or Pin the Tail on the Donkey, remember there will still be some children in this age group who are nervous, so don't force them, and always use a soft blindfold such as a scarf. An airline sleep mask is ideal.

Do-it-yourself activities

You might like to try some do-it-yourself activities, too, specially for winter parties when you are more confined. Try letting the children make their own party hats before tea. Provide cut out strips of thick paper or card, plus glue sticks, and lots of pieces of colored paper, sequins, gift-wrap ribbon and anything else they can use as decoration.

Another fun but sticky activity is to get them to ice their own cookies. Provide plain ones, and little bowls of lurid colored glacé icing, plus lots of different decorations such as chocolate chips, colored or chocolate jimmies, chocolate threads or silver dragees. Leave the iced cookies (labeled with the name of the cooks) somewhere cool to set until the party meal.

Games for the three to fives

There are many, many games which you can play with this age group, while most of the ones they played when younger remain popular for a while yet.

Games for outdoors:
- hopping race
- somersault race
- three-legged race (use loose scarves or ties for safety)
- Stuck in the Mud – a kind of free-for-all tag in which the person who is "it" catches people, who then have to stand still with their legs apart until "released" by another child crawling between their legs
- Beat the Ball – in which the children have to try to get to the end of the back yard before a ball (a fairly heavy one, like a basketball) that you roll along the ground.

You could even set up a little obstacle course consisting of things to jump over, climb on to and wriggle under.

Indoor games:
- Musical Chairs/Statues/Hats
- London Bridge
- The Farmer in the Dell
- Here We Go round the Mulberry Bush
- On the Farm – in which you tell a simple story involving various farm animals, and every time you mention one of them the children have to make the relevant noise
- Balloon Bouncing – the children have to try and keep a balloon up in the air for as long as possible
- Pin the Tail on the Donkey.

Pre-school parties are a lot of fun but at the end of the day you may find the little host or hostess is very tired. Expect tears and a terrific feeling of anti-climax – but also requests for another party "tomorrow" – the ultimate accolade!

Six to Tens

The secret of successful parties for school-age children is to be one step ahead all the time. Children from six to ten are lively and fun-loving, but their energy needs to be directed if they are to enjoy themselves and not become bored. Draft in lots of help, and have a strict mental timetable of events, then everyone (including you) is going to think it's "terrific"!

The conventional party, with games and a celebratory meal, can continue to give pleasure to school age children – all you have to do is make the games more sophisticated. But you can also introduce lots more inventive ideas as well, as the children themselves are more receptive and creative, and the older they are the more they will want to do for themselves.

However, after about the age of seven, you yourself may want to bring conventional home-based parties to a temporary halt. Your children and their friends will be growing at an alarming rate and seem to take up twice as much room as they rush about, and your home suddenly seems rather small when you contemplate a dozen eight- or nine-year-olds in your living room. This is when you can start thinking about parties somewhere else, or which involve an activity away from the home with only the meal back at base.

Throughout childhood (indeed throughout life) birthdays are the major reason for party-giving. Once the children go to school you will find the guest list lengthens as your child tries to invite everyone in the class, plus the best friends from the swimming club, the scout group *and* all those children they met at camp last year.

This calls for negotiation – maybe you can accommodate them all this year in the local community center on condition that next year it's a visit to the movies with three close friends only!

Timetabling

If you are going to give a big party, either at your own home or in a rented hall, you need to plan the timetable carefully so that there is no moment when all the children are wondering what to do next. (It's at times like this that you realize what heroes school teachers are!) Don't make the mistake of making your party too long – two to two and a half hours is quite long enough for you and the children to get enjoyably exhausted!

Much depends on the time of year. If it's winter and the party has to be inside, the games and activities must be geared to the size of the room. This is when acting and guessing games can be a boon. If it's summer, make every effort to get everyone outside and organize as many races and team games as you can think of – despite running around frenetically children of this age never seem to tire of them!

Spend at least the first hour playing games so that everyone has a good appetite and is happy to sit down for a while to eat. If you're having an entertainer (and this is an excellent idea in the winter months for this age group) it's quite a good idea to have the show *after* the meal. Find out how long the entertainment will take when sending out invitations and fix the finishing time of the party accordingly.

Special planning for Christmas

Thinking ahead is essential for parties at popular times of the year like Christmas. For instance, for a typical Christmas party to be visited by Santa Claus, you'll need to recruit a suitable male friend to act the part about four weeks before so you can fix the date of the party and reserve the Santa costume in good time. Send out the invitations about three weeks beforehand, having decided the time and duration. It's particularly nice to have a late afternoon party at Christmas or New Year so that

the Christmas Tree looks its best and Santa can arrive after dark.

Christmas calls for a special cake. Fruitcake is traditional, but not all children like it. Instead, make a cake in the form of a tree or in the shape of Santa (cut from a large sheet cake) and decorate it appropriately with colored icing. Up to three days before, make as much party food as possible and refrigerate or freeze it in preparation.

Remember to buy and wrap little presents and put them in a suitable sack to be delivered to the chosen Santa Claus so he can bring it with him on the day. Having a Santa Claus to call makes it even more essential to have a fairly rigid timetable of

events for the party itself. You will have to arrange a precise arrival time with him (say, five o'clock) and then have the refreshments finished and cleared away ready to receive him.

You'll also need to make sure you have enough balloons, crackers, paper plates and cups to go around everyone. This is particularly important if the party is to be on Christmas Day itself or the Sunday before, when all the shops are usually shut.

Games and gifts
Whatever time of year, decide on the games you are going to organize and make a list – you may well not get through them all but it helps when your mind goes

Make food colorful and imaginative: Cheese and celery "boats", sausages in bacon and potato chip cookies.

blank and there's still half an hour before going-home time! Assemble all the equipment you need for games well before hand – if there's going to be bobbing for apples in the back yard, make sure the bowls and apples are ready; if you're doing a guessing or memory game which needs pencils and paper, make sure you've got enough of both.

For a birthday party or a Christmas party, or any other festival, many of the guests may arrive with gifts for the small host or hostess. You need to have a policy for this: Either allow time at the beginning of the party for each gift to be opened individually as it is given, or agree with your child that all the presents will be put aside until the end (or even after the guests have departed). This latter course avoids an unseemly scrabble from one gift to the next, with your child scarcely knowing what has been given. It also allows you time to make a proper list for "thank you" notes afterward.

Suggested party timetable

In the morning: Prepare fresh foods and decorate the house. Seven-to-ten year olds usually love helping with this so one of your helping adults (perhaps a handy grandparent) could organize this. It also helps to fill in waiting time.

2.00pm: Guests start arriving, perhaps bearing gifts.

2.15pm: Start the games. Aim to alternate energetic games with more sedate sitting down ones, perhaps involving pencils and paper. If you're having energetic games, especially in the summer, have a break for drinks all around after the first half hour.

3.00pm: Sit down to the party tea. If it's a birthday, bring the cake on last with candles for blowing out and the ritual singing of "Happy Birthday". For Christmas and other festivals, have the cake as a centerpiece, but again, don't cut it until the end. Some children won't even want a piece by then, and you can ask one of your faithful helpers to cut it into portions for distributing at going-home time.

3.30pm: If you're having an entertainer, or perhaps a visit from Santa Claus, or the Easter Bunny or whoever, he or she can arrive at this point. Everyone can then sit down after the meal and

relax for a bit. Have another game up your sleeve in case the entertainment finishes before the allotted home time.

5.30pm: Parents arrive to collect their offspring. It is a sociable gesture at Christmas time, or even at other festivals, to offer them coffee, tea or a drink (if not driving), though don't let this distract you from the farewells. Your child can distribute pieces of cake and small gifts as the children leave.

Games for winter parties

Even if you introduce new games, include a few favorites to avoid disappointment:
- Hide and Seek
- Wheelbarrow Race
- Musical statues
- London Bridge
- Red Rover
- My Grandmother Went to Market
- Charades
- The Hokey Cokey

Outdoor summer parties

If you're giving a party in the summer, either at home in your garden or out in the park, you can be a lot more casual than in winter. Invitations only need to go out two weeks ahead once you've decided on the place. If you are going out, enlist the help of at least two other adults to come with you so no one gets lost. Alternatively get everyone to rendezvous at a well-known spot. And make sure you've got a contingency plan up your sleeve, and everyone's phone number, in case it's wet!

If you're going to have a picnic party, pack the food into coolers and send someone on ahead with it, while you gather the guests together. An essential item is a really penetrating whistle, which everyone should be told is the signal to come together for meals, home time, or whatever.

Outdoor games

- slow bicycle races and bicycle slalom (make sure everyone brings a bike)
- Mother May I?
- Bobbing for apples
- Chain tag
- Three-Legged Race, and Four-Legged Race to be different (with children tied together in threes)
- Egg and Spoon Race (hard-boiled eggs!)
- Passing the Orange from chin to chin
- The Frozen Spoon (make one spoon per team really cold by putting them in the freezer well before the party.Tie a very long piece of string to each. The teams have to pass the spoons up one sleeve across their backs and down the other of each person, so that they end up joined together — and very cold!)

Theme parties

Some children in this age group love dressing up, but a mixed group of boys and girls may be reluctant. However, you'll probably find that something easy

Children in this age group need little encouragement from their parents to dress in style for their parties, and may spend ages preparing.

like monsters or witches and wizards (ideal for Halloween), pirates, spacemen, or your child's favorite TV character (lots of choice here) will allow plenty of scope for both the very imaginative and the more reserved. Alternatively, a more abstract theme may appeal. This could be a color – red, blue, black or silver – or the theme could be music, or books, or movies. Here are three ideas for themes and how they can be carried out:

A red party

Have red decorations, tablecloths napkins, plates and cups. Dress the children (and yourself?) in red clothes and red party hats. Paint their faces red with face paint. For extra sophistication, install red light bulbs – but keep plain ones in some lamps as red bulbs do not give out a lot of light.

You can provide red food with tomato and red pepper pizzas, red jelly, a red cake with bright red icing, strawberry shortcake, homemade raspberry ice cream, and cranberry juice or cherry cola to drink.

A musical party

Decorate the room with big murals of notes, staves, and other musical symbols, and with cardboard cut-out musical instruments.

Make a cake in the shape of your child's favorite musical instrument. You can buy a special musical candle from a novelty store to put on it; it will play a tune when it has burned down to a certain level.

Get the children to dress up as musical instruments.

Organize square dancing or get someone to play a musical instrument during the party, and play musical games such as

Musical Bumps, Musical Statues, or Musical Forfeits (if they move when the music stops they have to sing a song or answer a question on music).

An indoor garden party

Decorate the room with flowers and leaves made and painted by the children.

Ask the children to come in flower or plant motif fancy dress, and provide flower or leaf garland party hats.

Cut sandwiches and make little cakes in flower and leaf shapes. Make a cake to a garden design, and make chocolate leaves and iced petals for the birthday or other cakes.

Play word games that involve flower and plant names, adapting familiar games as appropriate, such as X Marks the Spot (choosing a spot where treasure is buried in the back yard), or Flower in the Flower Pot (which follows the same principle as Pin the Tail on the Donkey, but uses an artificial flower and a pot).

Food for hungry party-goers

Children over about six have big appetites. While under this age the sheer excitement of the party and the luxury of so much choice may impede their appetites, over this age children have no such problems, especially boys. They are quite capable of eating just as much if not more than adults.

Although there's a temptation to provide exactly what the junior host wants as it's his or her party, there's no need to be confined to burgers and fries. If you make it look fun, you'll be amazed at what children will eat – even if – horror of horrors – it's good for them!

Food suggestions

Six- to ten- year olds are developing more catholic tastes in food, so offer a mix of favorites and novelties

- hot dogs split with Cheddar cheese fillings
- empanadas (spicy meat-filled turnovers)
- pizza slices with peas for eyes, grated cheese hair, button mushroom noses and ham mouths
- barbecued spare ribs
- chicken drum sticks
- real baked beans
- celery "boats" with cheese slices for sails
- potato salad

Passing the Orange is a good way of getting children together! They have to pass the orange around a circle without using their hands.

Sweet alternatives

Of course, no party would be worthy of the name for children if there weren't lots of delicious sweet treats, but it is possible to get away from the normal plates of iced cookies and brownies. Try meringue piped or molded into the shape of animals such as mice, snakes or crocodiles. Chocolate chip cookies cereals are ever popular – and they can be made by the children themselves without too much supervision. Ice cream is a must; offer two or three flavors. For a real treat make your own. Serve it in ice cream cones instead of bowls. Of course, banana splits or ice cream sundaes never come amiss. Or you could provide novelty by making ice cream clowns. For each of these, set a scoop of ice cream on a round chocolate cookie and invert a cone on top for the hat. Use chocolate chips for the face and hat bobbles, anchored in place with dabs of glacé icing.

Sweet foods don't have to be cold either, which is good for Haloween or a winter party at the ice rink or in the snow. Try toasted marshmallows or baked bananas, put in the oven in their skins, then opened and served with whipped cream. The skins go black but the flesh is warm and deliciously sticky. Chinese candied apples are different; they consist of pieces of apple dipped in boiling taffy mixture then quickly immersed in chilled water to set the taffy layer, while the apple inside is still hot.

Unlike with toddlers, it's always a good idea to over-estimate the quantities. If you're careful, most of any leftovers can be kept for another occasion, but you will also find that one or two things are particularly popular, so the extra are needed.

HOW TO MAKE PARTY HATS

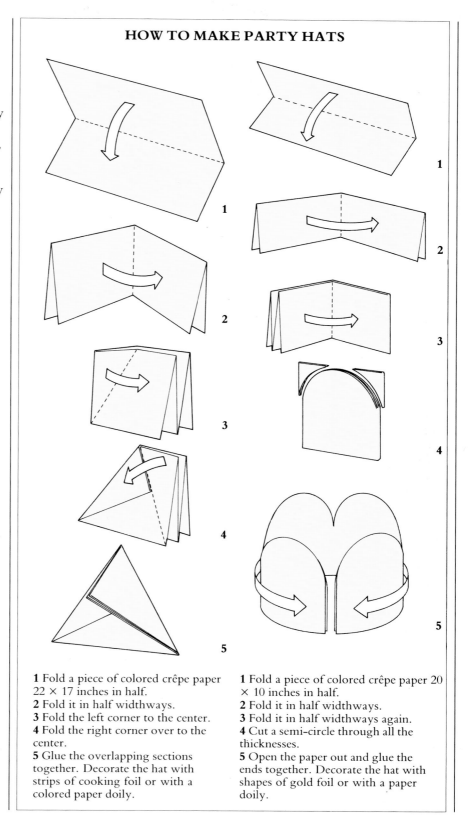

1 Fold a piece of colored crêpe paper 22 × 17 inches in half.
2 Fold it in half widthways.
3 Fold the left corner to the center.
4 Fold the right corner over to the center.
5 Glue the overlapping sections together. Decorate the hat with strips of cooking foil or with a colored paper doily.

1 Fold a piece of colored crêpe paper 20 × 10 inches in half.
2 Fold it in half widthways.
3 Fold it in half widthways again.
4 Cut a semi-circle through all the thicknesses.
5 Open the paper out and glue the ends together. Decorate the hat with shapes of gold foil or with a paper doily.

The Pre-teens

Once your children go into double figures, they begin to look on themselves as mini-teenagers — little streetwise sophisticates who want a bit more than games and birthday cakes with candles at their parties. However, at this age they are often only too happy to help do the organizing themselves, so parties begin to be real joint efforts.

Girls and boys at this age often have different ideas about what they consider to be a good party, and sometimes it's difficult to get them to invite a mixed group. But one of the most popular and in many ways easiest options is to run a disco.

Braving a disco
If you're on good terms with the neighbors and you've got enough room for dancing, rent the equipment and set up the disco in your own home. If you think it might be too noisy or you simply haven't got enough room, rent a local hall instead. There are lots of companies that hire out this sort of equipment, and you can find them in Yellow Pages or the local paper, or ask someone who has hired one before. What it usually involves is two turntables or tape decks, a microphone for the DJ and a panel with lights, which are probably sound-sensitive.

Some companies provide their own DJ. This can be quite a good idea as the person concerned can often liven up the party, especially if there are a number of youngsters who don't know each other very well or who seem reluctant to dance. Alternatively, you could take on this role yourself or draft in an older

brother or sister who might otherwise find the whole occasion a bit of an intrusion.

It's good fun, too, for the kids themselves to have a go at deejaying. Give them, say, five minutes or three records to introduce, and then have a vote on who was the best. You can award

---

Disco game ideas

Forfeits can be popular with the pre-teens, giving chances to show off. There are two types that are suitable, Spot Forfeits and General Forfeits.

For Spot Forfeits, shine a powerful spotlight or flashlight over the dance floor then focus on one child, stop the music and make them do a forfeit — such as singing the current number one hit, doing a headstand, or patting their head and rubbing their tummy at the same time.

In General Forfeits the DJ calls for anyone to stop dancing whose name begins with "B", or who's wearing something green, or didn't go to school last Friday, or whatever. He eliminates people through various rounds of this and then awards a prize to whoever is left at the end: The prize could be to act as DJ for the next few records.

prizes or have Olympic type medals to hand out to the top three.

Whether it's you or a professional, having a DJ at a pre-teen disco is one way of introducing games, through the back door as it were! Eleven- and twelve-year-olds may think games are beneath them, but being made to do funny things by a presentable young DJ is another matter!

For this age group it's more grown up to have the disco party in the evening and it can start and end a bit later than normal parties. But make sure all parents are aware of the finishing time.

Disco food and drink

A disco party can be three hours long without any difficulty because the children enjoy dancing and have lots of energy. But make sure there's plenty to drink all the way through – dancing is thirsty work. Provide a proper "bar" serving not only the usual soft drinks like cola, lemonade and fruit juices, but also some special "cocktails" or mixed drinks which add to the party atmosphere. The food needs to be sustaining but light; it isn't very comfortable to hip-hop with your stomach full of pasta or pastry.

Food and drink should look that much more grown-up for this age group, but that need not prevent a sense of fun in the presentation.

Provide easy-to-eat salads such as coleslaw, three-bean salad, or Waldorf salad with apple and walnuts and potato salad. Bacon and sausage kebabs go down well, using rolled strips of bacon and cocktail sausages, served with warmed Greek pitta bread, rather than hamburgers. Pieces of pizza are always popular, as is hot garlic bread (provide lots of paper napkins with this). Chicken drumsticks perhaps served with a spicy barbecue dip are easier on the stomach than heavy hamburgers, and you can round off the meal with a deliciously light fruit compôte or mousse.

Basic mousse recipe

two packets of flavored gelatin
boiling water
2 × 14.5 oz cans evaporated milk,
chilled
1 cup whipping cream,
whipped

Prepare gelatin as directed on the packet. Leave to cool but not set. Whisk the evaporated milk until thick, then whisk into the Jello. Fold in the cream. Turn into bowls or molds and chill until set.

You can use any flavor of Jello and add various suitable flavorings or garnishes such as marshmallows, raspberries or other berries, angelica, nuts or mint chocolate chips.

Other party ideas
Your child may want a smaller, more intimate party than a disco. Girls particularly like the idea of getting together with a small group of like-minded youngsters and just doing exactly what they want to do. Why not then suggest

A carriage birthday cake for a girl, with meringue "caterpillars".

Disco drinks

- Fawn's Fizz: Equal measures of fresh orange juice and soda water, garnished with slices of orange
- Ruby Punch: Equal measures of cranberry juice, clear apple juice and soda water, garnished with thin slices of lemon
- Apricot Cooler: Blend 1 quart of orange juice with 6 canned apricot halves, then mix in 1 quart of 7-Up; serve in a pitcher well-chilled with ice cubes
- Pony's Neck: Mix 2 parts of clear apple juice to 1 part ginger ale in a picher with ice cubes. Garnish the mixture with thin slices of red apple, de-cored but unpeeled.

a slumber party? Get your daughter to invite not more than six friends and turn her bedroom into a dormitory for the night.

Sleeping bags on the floor are the order of the day, plus lots of magazines, the TV, a cassette player and the favorite pop cassettes, and lots of tasty bedtime snacks. The bedroom is strictly out-of-bounds to all other members of the family. If they're still chatting at midnight simply bang on the door and leave them to it!

Rather than simply taking boys to watch sport passively, you could try taking them somewhere where they can get "hands on" experience of an activity they might not normally have access to – such as wind-surfing, kite-flying or grass skiing. This sort of

outing might be popular with girls, too, or a mixed group.

For little trendsetters, why not give a proper dinner party, with everyone dressed up to the nines, three or four courses, a properly set table, candles, flowers – the works! And to crown it all, mother and father don apron and dark suit and act as waiters.

Junior dinner party timetable

Two weeks ahead, send out invitations – the classier the better. Make sure the guest list is no more than eight including the host or hostess. You may need to rent a proper waitress's black dress and frilly apron and cap, and a dinner suit for the waiter; if so, reserve them at least a week ahead.

Consult with your pre-teen host and fix the menu, pre-cooking and freezing as much as possible. On the day, set the table with your best crockery and cutlery, tablecloth and napkins. Decorate with flowers, and put out place cards (see pp. 47–9).

When the guests start arriving at 6.00pm or so, father or perhaps older brother can act as butler, taking coats and announcing the guests, while mother or older sister hands around drinks such as Fawn's Fizz or mock champagne (white grape juice and soda).

At 6.30pm usher everyone into dinner with as much formality as possible (it may well reduce the guests to giggles), then serve the dinner as haughtily as possible. When everyone has finished organize games until whatever finishing time you have set out on the invitation.

> ### Dinner party menu
>
> Choose one from each course:
> - gazpacho; lightly curried shrimp vol-au-vent; ham, yogurt and cottage cheese dip with crudités; shrimp cocktail; avocado with grapefruit segments
> - broiled minute steaks; breaded sole fillets; roast chicken marengo; Swiss cheese soufflé
> - french fries; sautéed potatoes; new potatoes
> - cut green beans; corn; mixed salad
> - meringue baskets with whipped cream and raspberries; strawberry shortcake; real chocolate mousse; homemade ice cream

FAMILY CELEBRATIONS

Although the mechanics, food and drink may be similar, family parties have quite a different atmosphere from others. Protocol and the desire to put on an impressive show are never so prominent when the guests are mainly or entirely family members, and, of course, there is no worry about people not knowing each other and having to be introduced.

This does not mean, however, that the major family occasions do not admit people from outside the precious inner circle of blood ties. Christenings and wedding anniversaries can, in fact, be major social occasions with a large number of guests, but they do tend to be limited to close friends of the family; these are hardly the occasions to get to know the school principal.

It is the major milestones in life that get marked by family parties – a coming of age, say, or a new arrival. Most of them are traditionally held in the afternoon or at lunchtime, perhaps because of the age groups involved. The afternoon is also popular because of the special status of The Cake, which is the featured attraction of the refreshment table.

Nowadays champagne is also increasingly coming to be be regarded by many people as an essential part of any major celebration.

The combination of cake and champagne is typical of get-togethers in celebration of some major family milestone.

Christenings

A christening is a wonderfully joyous occasion, involving the family and your closest friends. But whatever you do, party provisions are never going to come better than a poor second in terms of attracting attention.

The time of day at which christenings are held varies. Some churches conduct them as part of the regular morning service, while others arrange a special afternoon ceremony. But the essence of the party afterwards is the same.

As many of the adults invited will be siblings or friends of the parents they will be of child-rearing age too, so there will normally be plenty of children present. And as christenings are all about a child, they are events to which children themselves can easily relate.

For this reason, it is best to serve food that all ages can enjoy: sandwiches, rather than fork food, and cake and cookies or ice cream rather than a more sophisticated dessert.

Preparing the table
Unless the number of guests is too great for the space available, home is both the most practical and the most welcoming place for the party. However, not much can be left to the last minute, as host and hostess will be much concerned with looking after the baby. Cold food, prepared in advance, is the only practical option, unless you hire professional caterers. Set the table well before going to the church.

Go for variety in the food, in both flavor and appearance.

Not only is a mix of sweet and non-sweet essential, but so are changes of texture: not all the sweet things have to be smooth, for example. Changes in appearance merely require a little thought in the finishing: two plates of mixed rye bread and

> ### Catering with sandwiches
> - Make a good variety of fillings.
> - Use different types of bread.
> - Garnish plates with sprigs of herb and slices of tomato, cucumber, etc.
> - Cut sandwiches small, and into different shapes.
> - Slice bread thinly.
> - Cover to keep fresh.

white bread sandwiches look better than one of each. Smoked salmon, ham, and other flexible fillings can be served rolled in bread to form pinwheel sandwiches. Sweet breads such as date-nut bread can be cut thinly and the slices overlapped in a circle.

The christening cake
Real traditionalists may already have taken care of the cake, because the ancient custom was to reserve the top tier of the wedding cake for the christening of the firstborn. However, it is much more likely that you will be making a cake specially.

Whether the christening cake is a rich fruit mix or a sponge is a matter of taste – but make something that will not quickly go stale if you are planning to send pieces by mail to anyone who could not come on the day. Whichever base you go for it should be beautifully decorated with a rich icing and incorporate the name or initials of the child.

The provision of a christening cake does not preclude making other cakes, such as chocolate cakes or angel food – surefire hits with all the children and with many of the adults too.

Displaying the gown
Christening gowns are often finely worked garments that are passed on from generation to generation. Once the baby is home he or she will be put into something practical, but leave the gown on display for the guests to admire. Put out the presents in the same place too. This not only lets people view them, but also particularizes the celebration.

Christening gifts and accessories displayed to greet the guests. Pride of place is given to the gown; to its right is a cradle cover and a cradle toy, and above it a celebration tablecloth. The bouquet was made for a pew end.

Coming of Age

The moment one officially becomes an adult is a major event for everybody, and as a truly once-in-a-lifetime occasion calls for a very special form of celebration.

Many of the major celebrations in life, like weddings and christenings, have developed certain routines and conventions. But apart from the cake a twenty-first-birthday party has no set form. It is very much what one wants it to be, from a small dinner for the immediate family to an enormous all-night party involving more than a hundred people. Only personal inclination determines its nature and invention its shape.

There can be conflicting demands between peers and parents, between the desire for an epoch-making bash with lots of friends and a family get-together over good food. The answer to this is to go for both, with a family meal on the day, followed by an informal party for the hordes of friends on a nearby weekend.

The gathering of the teens
Whether you just vacate the family home for an evening (see pages 38–41) or rent a hall, you will want to make the party different. One certain way of doing this is by providing live music. Don't assume that the band has to make exactly the same sort of sound as is always on the stereo, as the strong allure of live music is itself a bonus. No band plays without breaks and the disco records, or whatever, can come in the intervals. On the other hand, a

TEMPLATES FOR PATTERNS ON FESTIVE CAKES

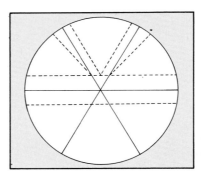

1 Wedges – fold a paper circle into sixths, and open it out. Mark lines one fifth way up from center and draw triangles from each to edge. Center panel is to ice name.

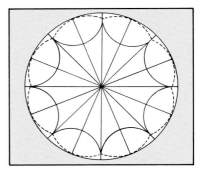

2 Curves – fold a paper circle into eighths, and in half again. Mark point about one tenth in from edges. Draw curves either way between them, with apexes on folds.

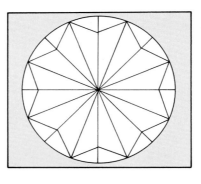

3 Star – fold a circle of paper into eighths. Fold each in half again. Mark point a quarter way down each side and draw lines to each from where center fold meets paper edge.

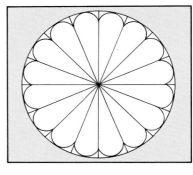

4 Heart – fold paper circle into sixteenths. Mark a point about one sixth way down on each edge. Join them with regular curves whose tops just touch the edge of the paper.

jazz band in striped blazers and straw hats will look great, but your son or daughter may well not agree to your hiring it if their real passion is Heavy Metal.

Otherwise, if you are keeping to home, hire a light show or run a film in one of the rooms (not a video; the flickering film is much more romantic and out of the ordinary). Old musicals go down especially well. Arrange a large board with a selection of photographs of your son or daughter's life to date, though the selection most definitely has to be mutually agreed.

Away from home

The alternative to home does not have to be the local community hall. There are plenty of other interesting, if more expensive, venues – a riverboat, for example, or a nightclub. Most owners of large spaces are looking for ways to defray their costs, and you may find by asking that you can rent a room in a local museum or a theater club, or even take over a restaurant. If you want to get away from it all you can sometimes rent barns - why not have a barn dance?

Marquees are not just for summer; they soon warm up and can be a way of introducing an unexpected outdoor flavor into a spring or autumn party. For a summer party, move the whole thing out of doors and make it a garden party.

If the budget runs to it, have waiters going around with trays of food and drink – nothing makes a person feel important more than having other people serve them. You don't necessarily have to have professionals, but if you take on paid amateurs, rig up some uniform for them in order to gain maximum impact.

The love of dressing up starts young and continues to old age. Even in the family home with the rugs rolled up, an extra sense of occasion can be provided by specifying evening dress – the further you put your hair up, the more you can let it down!

The family occasion

For the intimate family gathering, this can be the time to go out to a top restaurant. Some make a specialty of occasions, and will usually make this apparent in their advertisements in the local paper or Yellow Pages. There may be a small band or pianist, who will be only too happy to play "Happy Birthday" or a favorite song, though it is best first to assess honestly whether you risk

Letting your hair down is compulsory on reaching the age of majority.

never being forgiven because of the embarrassment caused.

The cake

A coming-of-age cake is an essential offering. The art is to produce one that is sufficiently elegant to appeal to the sophisticated young person. Don't bother with a novelty shape, although an "age" cake (see pp. 70–71) is still a good idea. Careful details and imaginative icing are now much more likely to be admired and appreciated. If cake-making is not your forte, order one from a good bakery. Money is better spent on precision work than on size.

Adult Birthdays

*Not all the fun has to go out of birthdays when you get older,
but the real enjoyment for busy adults comes from not having
to do the work but having it all arranged for them.*

If you are going to organize your own birthday party, then you can have just whatever you want, and choose the one of the informal or formal parties given in this book that most appeals to you. Alternatively, you might just hand it over to your family and let them treat you. There is, though, another kind of party that they might arrange for you in which *you* will definitely have no prior involvement. If you are the one with the birthday, read no further!

Surprise, surprise!
When organizing a surprise party for your partner, enlist copious help from friends to avoid too much elaborate subterfuge at home. The first thing to do is to erect the smokescreen, such as pretending to reserve a table in a restaurant, or inviting a couple of close friends over for dinner.

Providing the drink needn't be much of a problem as it can be collected at any time in advance. You may have some suitable hiding place at home, otherwise it has to be left at the home of one of your guests, and an ice-breaking supply brought around and shoved in a cupboard just before the closet starts.

Food is a greater problem, and here the only alternative to the help of a friend is a discreet firm of caterers who will arrive with

everything ready on plates not a minute before they are required. Otherwise you need the time to prepare all the food in advance, and a nearby kitchen to do it in. If you simply don't have such time yourself, then a very good friend may come in as joint host and be willing to do the food for you, but you may have to do weeks of babysitting to repay the favor!

The final problem is getting your partner out of the house. If

Games

Party games are almost innumerable. Here are some proven favorites.
- Charades — in two teams, each person mimes a book, film, play or TV program title.
- Voice Over — everyone has to pick a record at random and mime the typical stage act of the (famous) singer to it.
- Are You There Moriarty? Two people lie blindfolded on the floor and try to hit each other with rolled-up newspapers.
- In the Manner of the Word — one person leaves the room, and the others decide on an adverb. When he comes back they act according to the word chosen and he has to guess what it is.

he or she can be relied on to come back from work at a specific time, have everybody waiting then, but otherwise you may be able to rely on a request to them to go to the liquor store or an urgent "unexpected" call from a friend to help rescue their cat. If you cannot rely on the success of a ploy like one of these, then you will just have to ask all your friends to besiege your home at the same time. If on the other hand, you can get your partner out for long enough, the traditional thing is to use the time to get all the guests hiding behind the furniture, or assembled in a darkened room with drinks in their hands. Well, it always works in the movies!

A family affair
Even a quiet family celebration can still be a party. The essential for the celebrant is to be pampered — no cooking or cleaning up, and your favorite food and drink. Young children might not be able to do a lot in the way of preparing the lobster thermidor or mixing a vodka martini, but they can help with making their own personal presents, blowing up balloons, acting as waiters, or putting on a little play.

A bit of pampering will get the birthday adult into the mood.

Golden and Silver Weddings

*Wedding anniversaries are normally private affairs,
quietly celebrated by just the couple concerned. However,
golden and silver wedding anniversaries happen on quite
a different scale. They are very special occasions, when
the whole family and close friends usually get together.*

The gathering of the clan in honor of its oldest members can be a massive occasion, calling for considerable organization. Fortunately, all adult members of the family should have been aware of the event's approach for a very long time in advance, so at least everybody should have been able to make sure that they are available.

Wedding anniversary parties are usually given by one of the offspring, and can be held either in his or her home or in the couple's. Although the couple will not in these circumstances be the hosts, they will all the same naturally think of it as their party, so negotiations should be held well in advance about who is going to be invited – whether it is just family or is to include friends as well. Solicit the help of any siblings too, as it is quite possible that they too will want to feel that they are giving the party for their parents.

Timing the party
The afternoon is usually the best time for the party. Young grandchildren may well not be up to lasting through the evening and will have to be taken home. Even if the anniversary couple themselves are still raring to go

into the small hours, the middle generation of parents may well be flagging if the evening is allowed to run on! If you do decide that the age distribution is such that a dinner celebration is right, still bear in mind the stamina of the key participants and go for an early starting time.

Providing for all generations

Produce a good range of foods popular with all ages, with sandwiches, rolls, biscuits and

cakes. Devils on horseback – bacon wrapped round stuffed prunes – tend to be popular with all ages. As party organizers you are not in the traditional hosts' role as that is occupied by the anniversary couple, so you may be able to spare the time in the kitchen to produce hot food. However, usually quiches and salads are sufficient if anything more than finger food is thought necessary.

Remember that by and large older people are more conservative when it comes to food than the baby-boom generation, and that now is the time to give grandpa what you know he likes rather than urging him to be adventurous.

Golden confection

The high spot of the golden anniversary meal is the cake. It needs to inspire memories of the wedding cake 50 years ago, so make it appropriately rich. Elegantly iced decoration is definitely in order, but something less profuse and less frilly than on a wedding cake is more in keeping with the staider approach to life of advancing years.

Give the cake the glint of gold by setting gold dragees into the icing and by adding small bows made of gold ribbon and gold leaves under iced flowers. Set the cake on a gold-edged plate.

Making presents

Gold, naturally, is all you need give, if you can afford it, but if not try making something using gold-colored material. Children especially can feel they are contributing to the event this way. Gold lamé, for example,

A quiet restaurant table can serve an intimate party even better than home.

can be used to cover coathangers or scatter cushions. Look out for gilt photograph and painting frames, or else buy plain ones, rub them down, and repaint them with gold paint. Wrap the presents up in gold paper, or use lavish amounts of gold ribbon and golden bows.

Wedding anniversaries

Everyone knows the precious metals by which twenty-fifth and fiftieth wedding anniveraries are known, but less known are the materials which are associated with many other anniversaries.

1st Paper	13th Lace
2nd Cotton	14th Ivory
3rd Leather	15th Crystal
4th Fruit	20th China
5th Wood	25th Silver
6th Candy	30th Pearl
7th Wool	35th Coral
8th Bronze	40th Ruby
9th Pottery	45th Sapphire
10th Tin	50th Gold
11th Steel	55th Emerald
12th Linen	60th Diamond

Silver and ruby weddings

Not surprisingly in light of the youth of the celebrants, silver wedding parties go at a faster pace, and often the couple will host a buffet or a wine and cheese party. But this can still be the occasion to present them with a special cake. The principles are as for the golden wedding but change the dragees and any ribbons and leaves on the cake to silver, and put the cake on a silver platter.

For a ruby wedding change everything to red. To get a good red on the cake you will need to color the icing with an appropriate red food coloring. Add a few frosted rose petals.

SEASONAL OCCASIONS

Across the Western world, the passage of each year brings with it certain annual events that we look forward to and enjoy each time they come around. And although the festivals vary from country to country, the principle behind them is the same – celebration! Some festivals are primarily religious, others reflect the cultural and historical heritage of a country. But even the most serious of them have a strong element of enjoyment.

Some days are born for parties, such as weddings and christenings, and some have parties thrust upon them, purely because we want to have a party and they provide a convenient date. But these seasonal occasions have the power to achieve parties – New Year's Eve, The Fourth of July, Christmas can all pass by in style without your holding a party, but what excellent "hooks" they offer to hang parties on! They do not have the strong conventions of the great formal celebrations, but there is more to them than just doing what you please as in the party-for-the-sake-of-it. The various features and rituals of the season can be incorporated in many individual ways by the discerning host and hostess. A theme to the decor, a variation on the customary food, or often just a little imagination in adapting some old, familiar custom can turn a good party into one that is hugely successful.

A festive array of fruit punches to stoke up a party at Christmas or New Year.

St Valentine's Day

On a special day in the middle of the northern winter, couples huddle together to celebrate love itself. A party is only two people on Valentine's Day, and any gathering with three or more is most definitely crowded.

The setting is all-important. A quiet corner, low lights, gentle music and a pretty-looking table are the essential scenery for an intimate dinner for two.

No one ever needs reminding of the romantic effect of candles on a dinner table. They create a gentle cocoon of light from which the rest of the world disappears. A naked flame flatters the complexion and adds a warm glow to everything it illuminates. Use new candles only, as there should be nothing second-hand about Valentine's Day.

Table flowers

One further element is almost as important as the food itself – flowers. Normally the principle for dinner table flowers is that they should be discreet. Different guidelines apply on February 14, and for once they should impose themselves on the scene, playing a large part in the creation of a romantic atmosphere. As there will be only two at the table, they can stand to one side where they will not come between you.

Deep red roses are the flowers that most readily come to mind in thinking of love, but they may be too bold in color for the rest of the table arrangement. In this case consider pale colors that harmonize with the decor. Certain pink flowers endow the table with

an early touch of the coming spring, such as tulips, hyacinths, or ornamental cherry. This is a time when scented flowers can be appropriate at the table.

The language of roses

For the Romans any rose was a symbol of Venus, goddess of Love. Only modern usage particularly links the red rose with passion, but traditionally different varieties have special meanings.

- white rosebud – too young to love
- Moss rose – voluptuous love
- Provence rose – my heart is in flames
- China rose – beauty ever fresh
- yellow rose – infidelity (one to be avoided!)

Food

According to the anonymous but optimistic inventors of folklore, certain foods are supposed to increase the intensity of passion. But although there is no scientific evidence for their supposed aphrodisiac powers, lobster and oysters are still an appropriate treat.

How much of the meal you prepare in advance will depend on how well you know your partner. For a newer relationship choose

dishes that can be left by themselves in the kitchen while you enjoy a drink in the living room. Couples who have been staring at each other across the table for 25 years have no illusions about the work that goes into cooking, and might be content to save their romantic tête-à-tête until the food reaches the table.

Preparing oysters

SERVES 2

12 oysters
lemon
wholewheat bread and butter

Chill the oysters in the refrigerator for an hour and serve them on a bed of crushed ice.

Hold each oyster in a cloth by the larger of its two shells. Take a short sharp knife and prize the shells open, cutting between them with a see-sawing action. Any that open very easily are not fresh and should be discarded.

Squeeze lemon juice on the oyster flesh and swallow it in one go. Serve with buttered bread.

The most intimate party of all – a candle-lit supper for two, with spinach creams, lobster au gratin and a strawberry cake. The tall flower arrangement both complements the color scheme and enhances the romantic mood.

Passover

The eight-day celebration of Passover is one of the most important in the Jewish calendar. Like many Jewish festivals, the religious service is a family affair built around a meal which is very splendid and convivial.

Passover celebrates the freeing of the people of Israel from their slavery in Egypt. Various items will appear on the table which symbolize the misery of captivity and the joy of release. For example, hard-boiled eggs are served in brine, where the salt water stands for the tears shed in Egypt and the eggs for the new life to which the Israelites were escaping.

The prohibition on yeast

The Jews left Egypt in such haste that they were unable to bake their bread properly and instead had to make Matzot, or unleavened bread. Accordingly, no foods with yeast are allowed at all during the Passover, and the house will be searched the night before the festival begins for any traces of it. Matzo meal and potato flour are therefore common ingredients in Passover food.

All the food is, naturally, kosher, which among other things means that there is no mixing of meat and milk in any of its forms. In Orthodox Jewish households separate utensils are kept anyway for cooking meat and dairy products, but so special is the Passover that other sets of cooking utensils for each are set aside for use at this time of year only.

The prohibition of yeast extends to what is drunk. The traditional drink is wine which has been pasteurized to ensure that no trace of yeast remains.

Passover foods

Passover is a spring meal, itself symbolizing the new beginning as spring marks the return of the Earth to life, and hence features eggs in abundance, and lamb, the common sacrificial animal. Eggs feature in many dishes, such as Passover pancakes, which are cut into strips and boiled briefly, boobelach, a small pancake served with soup or meat, and matzo kleis, which are boiled onion balls. Eggs and matzo meal or potato flour also form the basis for many delicious desserts which can be served at this time, such as carrot pudding, orange cake and macaroons.

Another traditional dish is charoseth, which is symbolic of the building materials the Israelites had to use when slaves in Egypt. It consists of chopped almonds, hazelnuts or walnuts, grated apple and cinnamon, bound into paste with wine and shaped into flat rounds.

Jewish cuisine includes many excellent and distinctive ways of serving fish and poultry, a number of which are appropriate to this feast laid out here.

Gefillte fish

SERVES 4

2 lb mixed white fish, filleted and skinned
1 carrot
3 medium-sized onions
3 tablespoons matzo meal
1 teaspoon sugar
2 eggs, beaten
salt and pepper

Keep the head, skin and bones from the fish. Slice the carrot and one onion and cook them in water with the fish trimmings and some salt for about 20 minutes.

Chop the other onions, and mince the fish with them. Mix with sugar, eggs and matzo meal. Roll the mixture into 14–16 balls and simmer them gently for one hour in the stock. Remove the fish balls from the stock and put them on a plate. Strain the stock and serve it separately.

The fish balls can be fried instead of boiled.

There are several traditional elements to a Passover meal – the sliced eggs and the charoseth here by each place, and the central seder plate with its six items. All dishes must be strictly kosher, as with the borscht, fried gefillte fish, chicken with orange and almonds, and pineapple en surprise shown here.

Halloween

Dressing up for "trick or treat" and listening to ghost stories around a bonfire, children love Halloween. But it is not only children who have a taste for the ghoulish or who can enjoy a jack-o'-lantern; adults can join in the fun too.

Witches and wizards

The first essential for any Halloween party is dressing to the part. Black cloaks can be improvised from material and witches' hats made from black cardboard, though when it comes to transportation use a broomstick made of natural materials as colored plastic ones look as though they won't get off the ground.

Really to look the part also involves face painting, with bright red highlights around the lips and eyes and feline black streaks on the face. Or you could go for the ghostly look, painting the face deathly white apart from black or dark blue or green lips.

The witches' den

A darkened room with only jack-o'-lanterns looks spooky enough, though care has to be taken with candles, so place them well out of reach of small children. A few well-positioned spiders and bats, either hanging from the ceiling on threads, or positioned among the food, will produce suitable gasps. A visit to a novelty store should produce good large specimens that are guaranteed not to escape.

Cover surfaces such as tablecloths with black paper or fabric, and look for suitably gloomy paper plates and tablecloths.

Out of the cauldron

Eye of newt and tongue of frog are none too popular these days, so it is better to stick to hamburgers and hot dogs. Evenings can be cold at the end of October, so prepare warming food such as baked potatoes or a pot of chili, or a good thick vegetable soup. If you are wondering what to do with the insides of the pumpkin, then pumpkin pie is the answer. Candied apples also have their enthusiasatic adherents as a regular Halloween treat. For drinks give adults mulled wine and children a hot non-alcoholic punch.

How to make a jack-o'-lantern

Slice the top off the pumpkin. Run a sharp knife down the sides of the pumpkin flesh and lift out the fibers and seeds from inside, then scoop out the flesh with a spoon, leaving a thickness of about 1/2 inch under the skin and 1 inch on the base. (Reserve the flesh for a pumpkin pie.)

With a sharp knife cut a nose and eyes, working from the outside. Cut out a mouth, shaping a few scattered teeth.

Put a night light inside the pumpkin, light it and replace the top. After it has burned for half an hour see where the soot gathers inside the lid, and cut out a neat hole on the spot for a chimney. This will prevent the lid cooking and thereby shrinking.

Toffee apples

MAKES 14

14 short wooden sticks or skewers
14 medium-sized eating apples
1¹/₂ lb brown sugar
6 tablespoons sugar
2 teaspoons vinegar
2 tablespoons cornsyrup

Push a stick firmly into the core of each apple. Heat the remaining ingredients gently in a large heavy-based pan until the sugar has dissolved. Bring to the boil and boil for 5 minutes, until a candy thermometer registers 290°F, or until a little mixture dropped into cold water forms a hard ball. Brush the sides of the pan occasionally with a brush dipped in water to prevent crystals from forming. Remove pan from heat and place at once in cold water to stop cooking.

Tilt the pan slightly and dip the apples in one by one. Lift out and twirl over the pan until evenly coated with candy. Leave on an oiled cookie sheet to harden.

Preparing for Halloween can be almost as enjoyable as the party.

Thanksgiving

Thanksgiving is traditionally an occasion for a large family gathering. But many Thanksgiving dinners also include other guests – perpetuating the neighborly spirit that marked the original feast.

Although Thanksgiving is a distinctively American holiday – commemorating the occasion in 1621 when the Pilgrims thanked God for their first harvest and for having survived (barely) their first harsh winter – it also represents a much broader and older tradition of celebrating the earth's bounty. These English settlers were continuing a custom of their old country, the Harvest Festival.

The Pilgrims' celebration, however, had a special character. The presence of some friendly Indians at the table augured well for the colony's survival and was especially appropriate, as it was the Indians who had revealed to the English settlers that certain outlandish-looking items, such as pumpkins, cranberries and turkeys were edible.

The Thanksgiving feast
Today, the Thanksgiving dinner still revolves around two centerpieces, the turkey and the pumpkin. The turkey is, of course, roasted. For stuffing, traditionalists will insist on the breadcrumb, celery and sage version, to which coarsely chopped chestnuts may be added. However, you might like to experiment with one of the alternative stuffings described here. Cranberry sauce is the essential garnish; it can be made

MAKING A THANKSGIVING GARLAND

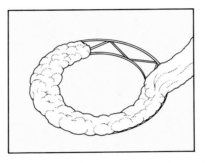

1 Cut 30 inches of heavyweight wadding into 6-inch wide strips. Twist two of them and place them inside a florist's wire ring of outside diameter 14 inches.

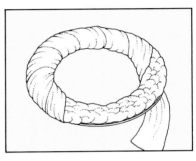

2 Wind remaining strips around outside of ring; catchstitch. Cut some 16-inch lightweight wadding into similar strips and wrap firmly round these; catchstitch.

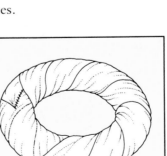

3 Cut a 40 × 45 inch length of brown polyester dress lining fabric into 6-inch wide strips. Wrap them around the ring to cover the wadding completely; catchstitch.

4 Wrap florist's wire round the ring first tightly, then loosely; secure separately. Tuck dried seed heads, fir cones etc under wire; stitch in place. Tie bows on wire.

even tastier with the addition of some grated orange peel.

For dessert, pumpkin pie is *de rigueur*. It is normally served hot, although some people prefer it cold. In either case, top if with generous dollops of whipped cream. For a variation, try the recipe below, which includes pecans.

To be thoroughly patriotic on this national holiday, choose a wine from California, Oregon or New York state. Red is generally preferred for turkey, though offer white wine or beer for those who prefer them.

Light pumpkin pie

SERVES 8

2 cups pumpkin flesh
zest and juice from 2 oranges
5 tablespoons sugar
2 medium eggs
10 inch pie crust, bakedblind
2 teaspoons ground ginger
20–25 pecan nuts
salt

Steam the pumpkin flesh until soft, about half an hour. Mash it and add orange juice and zest, sugar, ginger and salt. Chop two thirds of the nuts and add them. Heat oven to 350°F. Beat eggs, fold into the mixture and pour into the pastry. Spread remaining nuts on top and bake for 45 mins.

A touch of autumn

Although a trip to the garden will not produce the fresh flowers of spring and summer, fall has its portable beauties too. Those glowing russets and golds can be brought into the house or pinned in welcome to the front door in a garland of dried flowers, poppy heads, hazelnut cases and fir cones.

Stuffing the turkey

The following, mixed with onions, herbs, egg and breadcrumbs, all make the basis of fine stuffings:

- chestnut and apple, with egg and chopped pork
- chopped almonds, with ground ham
- lemon rind and juice, with ground pork
- chestnut purée, with sausage meat
- corn and honey, with chopped apple
- pecan nuts, with the heart and liver of the turkey
- oysters, with celery

A garland for the front door is a traditional Thanksgiving decoration, and a beautifully made home-made one will improve on anything you can buy. You can make one with dress lining fabric and material. To make it truly autumnal decorate it with what you find on a walk in your nearest woods, such as dried flowers, seed heads and fir cones.

Dried flowers come into their own now, but you can also decorate the house with naturally dried grasses, ferns, honesty, seed pods and leaves. Bowls or baskets of fir cones, apples and even seasonal vegetables maintain the air of autumnal fruition.

Christmas

As the nights get to their longest, we seem most to appreciate the company of lots of other people bent on a good time. Christmas parties need the least effort to get people to mix.

The party season reaches its climax in the approach to Christmas, so the first consideration is to get in early. However busy you are, aim to get out your invitations before Advent. The competition can be intense at this time of year, so make sure that your date is firmly inked in your guests' calendars before they fill up with other events.

A Christmas party *can* be just another cocktail party, plus a few balloons, fruit cakes, and inhibitions even lower than normal. But it is a shame not to do more than just nod to the season, when a little extra will produce a party that stands out.

Dressing the house
Despite the attempts of card manufacturers to make us believe that the hue of Christmas is the white of virgin snow, its real colors are red and green.

Put out green garlands with red ribbons on mantelpieces and tables, a green holly wreath on the door with red bows and plenty of berries, and red tablecloths with red and green napkins. Use red candles – but make sure they are secure and away from anything they could ignite.

Even if this is not to be its final resting place, on the day of the party put the Christmas tree in the window with the draperies open so that it puts guests in the mood as they approach your home.

Although they are ruinously expensive at this time, it is worth investing in flowers. Order them a

---

HOW TO CARVE A TURKEY

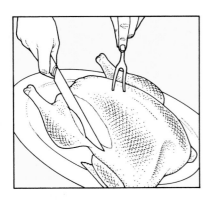 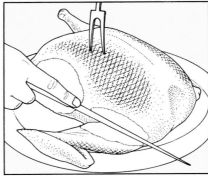 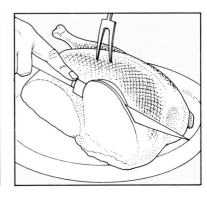

1 Leave the turkey to "set" for 10 minutes on a board or large plate with the breast facing outward. Remove a drumstick, and slice the meat from it.

2 Carve slices from the thigh and then remove the wings and strip the meat off neatly.

3 Carve thin slices from the breast. Serve a mixture of dark and white meat for each portion, plus slices of the stuffing. Finish carving one side before doing the other.

minimum of a week in advance, otherwise you may find you have simply missed the boat.

Dressing the guests

For a more extrovert type of party, invite everyone to come in costume – since Christmas is a time for children, perhaps as characters from nursery rhymes. Reserve is lower at this time of year anyway, especially after Christmas – not too many people will travel straight from the office dressed as Mother Goose!

Children receive gifts at parties whether Santa Claus is there or not, but why not give presents to adults too? You don't have to spend a fortune, and can, in fact, have a lot of fun choosing inexpensive gifts for people to be given as amusing mementoes.

Christmas cakes

In addition to the traditional mince pie that ends the Christmas dinner, you will probably want to bake a cake or two — especially for a party. Fruit cake is a perennial favorite; it should be made a month or two in advance so that the rum or whiskey will have time to soak well into the ingredients. You might like to give your Christmas a Continental touch with a Pannetone, a delicious light Italian cake available from some delicatessens. Or try a home-made boûche de Noël, a long fat French Christmas pudding that is a slowly cooked mix of chestnut purée, eggs, sugar and brandy served with a chocolate sauce.

There are many ways of decorating the home without recourse to streamers. This mantelpiece has a garland of seasonal greenery tied up with bright red ribbons, baubles, and a display of dried flowers and leaves. The stocking reminds children of who comes down the chimney.

The groaning board

If your party is on Christmas Day itself, or even on Christmas Eve, it will be built around the meal, with the customary fare. However, on other days standard party food is called for, with a few Christmas extras. Get in a good selection of cheeses, including some special ones like Camembert, Stilton (an English favorite) and Brie, and consider putting out some cold roast ham as an alternative to turkey.

The whole feeling of a Christmas celebration should be one of warmth, so there is a long tradition of serving a warm punches, though eggnog has many devotees. Don't forget, though, the drivers, so provide non-alcoholic beverages.

Mulled red wine

SERVES 9

1 bottle Cabernet Sauvignon
1/4 bottle inexpensive port
1 1/4 pints boiling water
sugar to taste
pinch of ground nutmeg
cinnamon stick

Heat the wine and port together in a saucepan, pour in the water and stir. Add the sugar, nutmeg and cinnamon, and serve hot.

Mulled ale

SERVES 10

2 pints dark beer
1/4 pints rum or brandy
3 tablespoons brown sugar
6 cloves
1 teaspoon ground ginger
pinch ground cinnamon and nutmeg
rind and juice of 1 lemon
rind and juice of 1 orange
1 1/4 pints water

Put all the ingredients into a large pan. Heat slowly, but remove before it boils, stirring continually to dissolve the sugar. Leave to stand for a few minutes. Strain into a warmed pitcher and serve.

■ **Note** Do not allow either of these drinks to boil while preparing them as the alcohol then evaporates. Stop heating them as soon as any steam appears and stir them for uniform temperature.

A Christmas crib will make a centerpiece to any party with children present. There is the bonus that your own children can help make it while you prepare the food and drink.

MAKING A CHRISTMAS CRIB

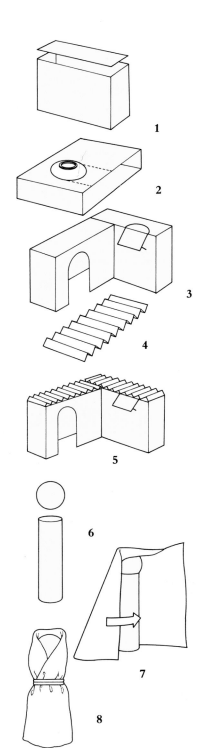

The stable

1 Take two small cereal boxes the same size. Cut one of the long sides off one.

2 Cut an archway in one of the sides of the same box, with its base on the side that has been removed, using a saucer to draw the curve. Glue a piece of blue transparent cellophane to the back wall opposite the archway, cut to the same shape.

3 Glue or tape the first box on to the end of the second, at right angles to it. Glue white paper towel over the walls and roof. Glue the whole stable to a large rectangle of card. When the glue has set firmly paint the walls white. For the canopy, cut a rectangle from some grey or brown gift wrap. Glue the end to the roof of the stable section. Color two matchsticks for support and glue to the outer edge of the canopy and the stable wall.

4 Cut two strips of red patterned gift wrap and fold concertina-wise.

5 Cut two pieces of pink crêpe paper to fit each part of the stable with the edges folded under. Glue to roofs.

Glue the folded red paper to each roof on top of the pink crêpe.

■ **Note** As an embellishment, cut another small door shape from brown paper and glue to the stable wall next to the archway. Make a large halo with a 4-inch diameter circle of gold paper and glue it to the stable wall.

A figure

6 Cut a piece of card to 4 × 2½ inches. Roll it round a pencil so as to make a tube about ½ inch

across. Glue a bead to the top of the tube as the head, at a slight angle so that it appears to be looking down.

7 Take a small colored paper napkin. Fold one edge under and arrange it over the bead head. Fold one side down in a triangle and across the "chest" to the back.

8 Fold the other side across it. Secure the robe with an elastic band. Trim off level with the bottom of the tube so the figure stands up.

■ **Note** For arms, cut shapes from the offcut and glue to the sides of the figure.

The donkey

9 Cut a piece of card 2 inch square and fold it in half. Wrap a piece of brown parcel paper around a small bead and secure it with an elastic band. Wrap and glue more paper over and round the folded card, turning the edges under.

10 Cut two long ears from the brown paper and glue them to the head. If they are too flimsy to stand up, cut the ears first in thin card and glue the brown paper to both sides.

Glue head to body. Color a short piece of string brown and glue it to the end of the donkey for a tail.

A palm tree

11 Cut a 4-inch square of card, roll it tightly and glue together. Color it brown. Glue to a small square of card.

12 Make a series of regular cuts along a length of green felt, to about half its width. Wind the uncut edge along the top of the tube, gluing as you go. Fan out the cut lengths.

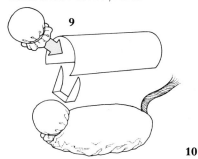

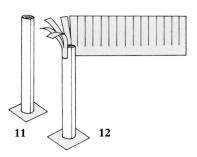

New Year's Eve

After the family-based celebration of Christmas, New Year is the time for friends, to "tak a cup o' kindness yet" so as to ensure that "auld acquaintance" are not forgot.

It goes without saying now that the year must begin on January 1, but it hasn't always been so. At various times it has been celebrated on Christmas Day, Easter Sunday, March 1 and March 25.

New Year customs

The ancient Greeks started a custom of giving presents at New Year, and in early medieval Britain you could bribe the local magistrate on New Year's Day! Nowadays, the gifts aspect of the festivity has been absorbed by Christmas. As a result, for New Year customs the English-speaking world turns to the Scots, for whom Christmas has remained a simpler, more religious festival, with the more flamboyant secular celebrations being held on December 31.

This does not just mean whiskey, but "first footing", the custom whereby the first person through the door after midnight should be a dark-haired man carrying coal, supposedly to bring prosperity for the coming year. The next part of the tradition is harder, for the house should be spotlessly clean, and all bills paid! The celebrations would continue well into New Year's Day, and even beyond. The front door would always be left open and anybody was welcome to enter and enjoy your hospitality and a "wee dram".

Ringing in the New

A more recent, and somewhat subconscious, custom relates to the crucial moment of the party, the turning of the year. Many people halt the party and put on the radio or television to watch the crowds in Times Square or another public gathering place welcome in the New Year. This practice extends the communal nature of the proceedings by introducing the feeling of joining the rest of the region in one big party.

Have the champagne ready, with bottles spread around to delegated openers if it is a large gathering so you are not spending the first ten minutes of the year filling glasses instead of hugging and singing. Because the party will have been going for some time already and thirsts well slaked it is definitely a waste to spend a lot of money on the best champagne you can find: the important thing is the pop and the fizz.

When you are preparing for the party, make sure that that there is a good uncluttered space for everybody to link arms to sing "Auld Lang Syne."

The last meal of the year

Whether it is a large buffet or just snacks, time the eating of the food so that it is well out of the way by midnight. As the normal starting time for New Year's Eve parties is around 9 pm, this means serving it at about 10.30. For most people this will be far later than they normally take their evening meal, so put out a plentiful supply of party edibles to keep them going. State "buffet" if appropriate on the invitation, especially if the starting time is after 9pm, so that guests don't arrive bulging with a prior dinner.

A turkey will be as welcome on a New Year's buffet table as at the Academy Awards ceremony, so resist all temptations to use up any left-overs. However, you may still want to serve up something special with a look of the old-fashioned to it, but that is not too heavy, in which case consider a roast ham. Keep up the contrast to the solid fare of Christmas with a good selection of salads and fruit or ice cream.

Spiced roast ham

SERVES 10

5 lb ham, boned and rolled
1 bay leaf
small onion, peeled
1 carrot, sliced
3 cloves
teaspoon black peppercorns
1½ tablespoons soft brown sugar
1½ tablespoons cranberry or quince jelly
1 teaspoon whole grain mustard
½ teaspoon allspice
¼ teaspoon ground coriander

Soak the ham overnight in cold water.

Drain and place it in a saucepan of cold, fresh water. Add the bay leaf, onion, carrot, cloves and peppercorns. Bring to the boil, cover, and simmer for 1½ hours.

Heat the oven to 425°F. Remove the ham from the water. Peel off the skin with a sharp knife, leaving the white fat. Place the ham in a roasting pan. Using a knife point, mark diagonal lines across the fat in a diamond pattern.

Mix together the sugar, jelly, mustard and spice. Rub this mixture into the fat. Bake the ham in the preheated oven for 30 minutes.

An array of solid winter food that rings out the ancient Christmas turkey with something suitable for the New Year. From left to right: bean and mushroom salad, roast chicken galantine, avocado and orange salad, and spiced roast ham. Traditionalists will insist upon the scotch whiskey, but red wine will accompany this fare equally well.

OTHER OCCASIONS

Large parties, whether formal or informal, are usually evening affairs, or else take place at weekend lunchtimes. But other times of the day are equally suitable for entertaining one's friends – in fact, from the breakfast gathering to the pajama party there is not a time of day that has not been put to good and regular use by party-givers. Such parties have their own, personal styles, for each part of the day has its distinctive mood and tempo.

Morning, afternoon and late-evening parties are more intimate and lower-keyed than the grand get-togethers, and during daylight hours coffee or tea is more likely to be the dominant beverage than alcohol. This does not make the parties in any way less sociable. On the contrary, sitting around an occasional table and eating muffins can be a far better way of talking to your friends than standing in a noisy room, bottle in hand. You can also feel that you are more truly welcoming people into your home as there is not the massive disruption of furniture involved with cocktail parties.

One of the joys of giving a coffee morning or a tea party is that you can provide food without the ritual of meat, fish and vegetable cooking. For the keen baker these are great times to show off your skills with the cake pan and icer, or to fill the house with the delicious smell of baking cookies.

A setting for a small, late evening supper party.

Breakfast

While you may never invite people especially for breakfast, if you have house guests over the weekend, this meal should match up to the high standard of the others you are cooking. You have the opportunity here to provide the most wonderful kind of old-fashioned breakfast one rarely has time for.

The Victorians are considered the champions of the large breakfast, and people today marvel at the robust constitutions they must have had. We forget that they would have been up for a couple of hours, and had done some work before sitting down to eat. The meal was also generally meant to keep them going until the early evening, as lunch was not a regular feature of the day.

The Victorians also had the advantage of having servants, who would have risen even earlier to prepare the food for them. Servants today are just not willing to start so early, so you will have to cook the meal yourself! It is therefore important to fix a leisurely eating time. Apart from saving you from starting before the lark, this allows both for those guests who want to linger in bed, and for those who want to emulate their nineteenth-century forebears to the extent of, if not actually doing the business accounts, at least going for an early stroll, run or workout.

Let the guests know the night before when breakfast will be served. This is not meant in the spirit of boarding house tyranny, but so that the hot dishes will be eaten hot, and because having everybody eat separately and then drift off is not a party. Nevertheless, put the hot dishes on warming plates for the inevitable Rip Van Winkles.

Serving breakfast
Even though the idea is for everyone to sit down simultaneously at the same table, breakfast is served as a buffet.

This custom started with Victorian philanthropy. The servants would not, naturally, eat with you, but it was considered unfair to make them wait for their first meal when they had already been up for so long. They would therefore partake of their lesser rations in the kitchen while the family upstairs helped themselves from the sideboard.

The practice is worth maintaining because a good hearty breakfast should offer a wide choice of dishes, with, for example, scrambled and fried eggs, grilled bacon slices, and sausages and French toast. Even if there is room to set it all out on the dining table, the food will get in the way of the guests, who will be forever passing to their neighbor. And those with delicate morning constitutions would inevitably find themselves by the glistening dish of bacon and sausages.

For the ambitious there are more elaborate dishes that can substitute for some of the staples: smoked salmon or trout instead of sausages, creamed or shirred eggs for scrambled, Parma ham instead of bacon, or for really fresh croissants and muffins, make your own.

The full breakfast menu

Ideas as to the best breakfast vary from one region to another. Here are some favorite items from which to put together an ample meal:

- several fruit juices, grapefruit, melon, fruit salad
- cereals, muesli, porridge
- pancakes, French toast or waffles
- bacon, Canadian bacon, ham, sausages, fried eggs, fried potatoes, scrambled eggs, poached eggs
- toast, croissants, biscuits, bagels, English muffins
- selection of jams, marmalade and honey
- coffee and tea

The following recipe is for a British dish that was invented in colonial India to produce something that seemed native. Despite its origin it is not spicy and makes a suitable dish for a formal breakfast.

Kedgeree

SERVES 6

1 lb smoked haddock fillets
½ pint milk
6 eggs
1½ lb long-grain rice
5 pints water
1 tablespoon butter
4 tablespoons chopped parsley
salt, pepper

Place the milk and fish in a large shallow pan and poach for 5–6 minutes, or until the fish flakes when pierced with a sharp knife.

Meanwhile, hardboil the eggs, then cook the rice in a large saucepan of boiling salted water for 12–15 minutes until just tender. Drain well and stir in the butter.

Strain the cooking liquid from the fish into the rice. Flake the fish, discarding any bones or skin. Heat the rice through over a very gentle heat and season with plenty of pepper and a little salt if required. Lightly fork the fish into the rice and reheat, stirring gently to avoid breaking up the fish.

Peel the eggs. Finely chop 2 of them and stir into the kedgeree with the chopped parsley. Pile the kedgeree into a warmed serving dish. Cut the remaining eggs into quarters and use to garnish.

Continental breakfast

The full cooked breakfast can often seem too much, possibly after a large dinner, or you may want a more informal meal, leaving guests to read the Sunday paper while they eat. The Continental breakfast offers a light alternative that is still

A Continental breakfast makes for a light informal start to the day.

different from the breakfast most people grab at home.

The basics are coffee and some form of bread. The coffee must be of a good quality– light or medium roasted beans freshly ground. For breads it is hard to beat lightly warmed croissants or brioches with a good-quality jam and unsalted butter. Fresh rolls are fine, providing they really are fresh – a stale lump of bread is a depressing start to the day. If you were in France you would have a baker down the road, but without that advantage, buy in advance some part-baked frozen French baguettes, and bake them in the oven. It does not take long, and you will also fill the house with the most appetizing aroma.

Coffee Mornings

Coffee mornings have become popular for fund-raising events, with everybody in the mood to speculate sums of money on the raffle, but even without the excuse of contributing to a worthy cause they provide a relaxed way to entertain friends without all the work and expense of a major party.

The style of coffee mornings balances between the formal and the informal. Their intimation of a life of leisure brings out the chic outfits and good-quality china and silver dessert forks. But they are also informal, with guests sitting in small groups on comfortable chairs and sofas.

At large functions people will not mind having to stand for at least some of the time, and the food can be served as a buffet, with plates of cookies scattered around the room. With smaller groups arrange the furniture into groups of three, four or five, with a coffee table (of course) or occasional table by each. Jealous eyeing of other tables will go on if you don't put out samples of all the cakes and cookies provided on each table. Also set milk or cream and sugar on each table, leaving you with only the coffee pot to circulate.

Cakes and cookies
Unless swamped with sugar, coffee has a naturally bitter flavor, which really needs to be balanced by sweet things to eat. This means tasty delicacies that appeal to the eye without overloading the stomach. Three little cup-cakes or cake slices per person should be more than

enough, but also provide an unlimited supply of cookies. Supermarket shelves offer a dizzying selection of cookies, but it is much nicer if you can make them yourself.

Shortbread

MAKES 6 OR 8

2 cups all-purpose flour, sifted
1 cup rice flour or ground rice
1 cup butter, softened
¹/₂ cup granulated sugar
salt

Put the softened butter and sugar into a bowl and cream with wooden spoon until light and fluffy. Mix the two flours and a pinch of salt to form a soft mixture.

Grease the bottom of a 9 inch quiche pan and put in the dough. Press it out evenly with your knuckles. With the back of a knife mark into 6 or 8 triangles. Prick through to the bottom of the pan with a fork in a neat pattern. Put the pan in the refrigerator to chill for an hour.

Heat the oven to 300°F. Bake the shortbread in the oven for 45 minutes or 1 hour until pale golden but still soft. Remove the pan and leave to cool before removing the cookies from it. Dust with sugar.

Instead of making a ring, before baking the mixture can be piped into fingers, stars or whorls.

Charity events

If you are hosting the event for your favorite charity, this will probably mean renting cups, saucers and plates. Some specialist china stores will rent out china, and as it is for charity you may not have to pay, other than for breakages. Help is essential, and should be on good supply, if

Coffee

Coffee comes in many different blends and flavors, so decide what you want, or even give a choice. Provide decaffeinated too, for those many people who have kicked the habit:

- Continental – dark, strong
- Kenyan – mild or moderate
- Blue Mountain – velvety flavor
- Colombian – lively
- Mocha – dark, very strong

only someone whose sole job is to go around replenishing empty cups. Unless you are a passionate cake-maker, rope in friends to make at least some of them for you, but do establish first what each person will provide, so that you do not end up with six chocolate cakes and nothing else.

A coffee party with a Continental touch – Linzertorte and a Dutch kerstkranz ring with German stollen and a Hungarian nut torte.

Afternoon Tea

There is something very comforting about eating an English tea around an open fire as the evening draws in. As a time for seeing friends, particularly those with children, it really comes into its own in winter.

In Britain tea is a concertina of a meal: you can squeeze it short with just a couple of light cakes or stretch it long with a fish or meat course, sandwiches, fruit breads, scones (biscuits) and a chorus line of cakes.

Generally the farther from the Equator you go, the larger it is. For the Scots, for example, tea is the main meal of the evening, and is expected to provide sustenance against the long cold night. Let your guests know in advance what to expect.

Blends and brews

The common feature of any tea party is the tea itself. Everybody has their favorite blend or brand, and there is no good reason to change yours just because people are coming over. Do, though, consider individual tastes, and make it quite strong with a pitcher of hot water at hand for those who prefer it diluted. Then ask people how they like their tea before you commit to the brim, and offer milk as well as slices of lemon.

But if you do want to branch out there are plenty of alternatives to a plain brew. The scented Earl Grey and green jasmine, the smoky Lapsang Souchong, and the delicate Orange Pekoe are all popular. Even British tea connoisseurs do not add milk.

Lastly, the fashion has grown in recent years for herbal teas, or tisanes. A wise hostess will include one or more of these in her offerings; they can be bought in bag form so a selection and the pitcher of hot water are all you need.

> **Tea varieties**
>
> Teas are often known by the area they come from, such as Assam, Darjeeling or Ceylon (as Sri Lankan teas are still called). All have their own distinctive flavor and strength. Specialist delicatessens or counters in big stores will describe them for you; otherwise there is often a description on the package.

Cakes and biscuits

Tea is a time for sweetness. This is recognized by the great masters of tea, the Japanese, who serve very sweet small cakes in their tea ceremony to offset the bitter taste of the green tea.

Black tea is not so bitter, but is still the perfect foil to cakes, muffins with jam, and cookies. A good tea party will have plenty of all of these, which is one reason why children like tea parties (except for the tea!). You can get away with bought cakes, but biscuits have to be fresh from your oven if they are not to taste doughy. Serve them on a dish wrapped in a napkin to keep them warm. A luxurious touch is to serve biscuits with whipped cream as well as the jam.

Plan the cakes and sweet spreads first and then give some thought to the sandwiches. Elegance rather than substance is the keyword here. Slice the bread and contents thinly, and show your generosity in the number offered.

For fillings offer two or three choices out of cold meats, cheeses, flaked salmon and egg salad, perhaps with some chopped watercress, and in summer the traditional thinly sliced cucumber. If there are to be children present the sweetness will spread from the cakes to the sandwiches, and extra plates with jam, peanut butter or banana sandwiches will be appreciated.

The full British tea starts with dishes that resemble breakfast: eggs, smoked fish, cold meats, bacon or sausages. These have to be eaten at table instead of off your knees, but are guaranteed to keep you going through the night.

A Scottish high tea is a complete meal: Grilled whiting with bacon and tomatoes, oatcakes, crowdie (a cream cheese), sautéed potatoes, scotch pancakes, Dundee cake and scones (biscuits).

Late Night Entertaining

A good evening out with friends should end in style. Going to a restaurant after the theater or a concert can be rather tense with both staff and guests keeping half an eye on the clock. But having the friends over for a late night meal at home is often easier and a lot more fun. If you plan it, there are many dishes that can be prepared beforehand, but should the impulse only strike during the evening, there are others that can be whipped up at a moment's notice.

Planning ahead

If you know that you are going to have people back after an evening out, have as much prepared in advance as possible. You no more want to come in from a pleasant evening and find you have a mountain of work to climb in the kitchen than you want your guests to have to wait for the midnight hour attended by the rumblings of their stomachs. This does not just mean having the food in a state of readiness, but having the table set, flowers arranged, candles put out ready to be lit, and any other room arrangements that you would make if you were having a dinner party.

A real fire is particularly cheering on a cold night. If you have an open fireplace build the fire before you go out so that with one match you can have your blaze on your return.

If you are going to serve red wine, leave it standing upright (to let the sediment sink to the bottom) in the room so that it is the right temperature when you come in. With white wine the normal advice on not overchilling

will have to be abandoned: It is far better to put it in the refrigerator before you go out and serve it at a lower than ideal temperature than to have to drink it warm.

Choosing the menu

Although none of you may have managed more than a light snack earlier in the evening, and appetites will be keen, late night food should not be too heavy. Avoid foods like roast meats that take a long time to digest, and particularly steer clear of very spicy foods which will haunt their consumers through the night. Avoid fried foods too, as they take a long time to pass through the system and can leave a lingering feeling of overfullness. Salads are usually preferable to cooked vegetables, but steer clear of the raw onions.

The best late evening food is something that you can cook earlier and reheat when you get in, or which can be left to cook very slowly while you are out. In the latter case this often means casseroles, but bear in mind the question of the heaviness of the

food; a fish casserole is a better choice than than a beef carbonnade. You can also, of course, take advantage of the time switch on your oven, but don't go for a dish where the exact number of minutes cooking is crucial. You might like the idea of coming in to find a nicely risen soufflé, but you won't be so keen if you are fidgeting in your seat when the play overruns, or shouting at oblivious traffic jams on the journey home.

If you have a completely reliable babysitter you can leave something in the oven and ask him or her to turn it on at a particular time.

The question of fast food is another reason for going for salads rather than cooked vegetables, as the vegetable that reheats well, other than in a casserole, has yet to be invented. Some people find that cheese at night gives them bad dreams, so if you put out the cheese board as the solution to the time problem, include some cold meats on it as well.

However, do not be so keen to produce food quickly that you throw it at your guests as they come in the door. As with lunch or dinner, give them time to enjoy a drink and to settle in before going to the table.

Just dessert

Forget the dreams of a Bavarian cream or a chocolate layer cake. The effort put into them earlier will not be fully appreciated as people's minds turn to going home, and their richness can even be off-putting late at night. A fresh fruit compôte is a better bet; it can be made as early as the previous day and be left to marinate happily in its own juices. Otherwise, dig some interesting ice cream out of the freezer.

Green fruit salad

SERVES 8

2 limes
1 cup water
³/₄ cup fine granulated sugar
¹/₂ cup white wine
1 small green-fleshed melon, such as Honeydew
2 cups seedless green grapes
1 firm pear
2 grapefruits
3 kiwi fruits
1 ripe avocado
2 Golden Delicious apples

Pare the rind thinly from the limes and cut it into thin strips. Put them in a saucepan with the water, bring to the boil and simmer for 5 minutes. Strain the rind; reserving both it and the juice, and make the juice back up to 1 cup with more water. Add the sugar, heat slowly until it dissolves and then boil it for 2–3 minutes. Add the wine and pour the syrup into a serving bowl.

Halve and de-seed the melon, and scoop out the flesh with a

Macaroni and tuna fish, served with a simple salad and an egg and walnut pâté as an appetizer.

melon baller, or cube it. Add it to the syrup.

Wash the grapes, removing any stalks. Peel, core and slice the pear. Cut away the peel and pith from the grapefruit and ease out the segments from between the membranes. Cut in half if large. Peel and slice the kiwi fruit. Add all to the syrup.

Squeeze the juice from the limes into a bowl. Quarter, peel and dice the avocado and toss it in the lime juice. Remove from the juice and add to the salad. Quarter, core and slice the apples and toss in the lime juice. Add apples and juice to the salad. Mix gently and chill. Sprinkle on the lime strips before serving.

The perfect appetizer

Soups fill the bill excellently in late night entertaining. They satisfy the immediate hunger pangs while the main course is cooking. They can be made well in advance, and if anything will improve for being left. In summer substitute a chilled soup, such as gazpacho or vichyssoise, for a hot one. An equally good alternative is to provide a cold appetizer such as pâté and toast, shrimp cocktail, deviled eggs, avocado (simply with a vinaigrette dressing or with a more elaborate filling) or prosciutto and melon.

The impromptu meal

It can happen at any time. Someone drops in unexpectedly or you have gone out in a group and no one has had time to eat beforehand. For such an occasion it pays to keep a stock of quickly accessible foods at home. If you have a microwave and a freezer it need not be much of a problem, and dishes as diverse as seafood pancakes and moussaka can be made during a spare evening and put in the freezer for just such an eventuality. There are also plenty of microwave cook books which will give you quick menus, and it is useful to be familiar with some of these.

But if you are microwaveless keep a supply of dried and canned goods that can be quickly turned into delicious dishes. Pasta is a great standby and lasts indefinitely; most pulses involve hours of soaking, but lentils cook quickly, and canned flageolets make an excellent basis for salads or hot meals; Chinese dried mushrooms reconstitute quickly in hot water; and canned tomatoes and tuna get the approval of even the most sniffy cookery experts. Keep a good collection of dried herbs for adding that essential extra.

The following is an example of a delicious dish that can be quickly conjured from larder to table.

Macaroni and tuna fish

SERVES 6

12 oz elbow macaroni
salt
1 tablespoon butter
1 large onion, peeled and sliced
1 garlic clove, crushed
1 teaspoon dried marjoram or oregano
2x7 oz cans tuna fish in brine, drained and roughly flaked
4–6 tablespoons plain yogurt

Sauce
4 tablespoons butter or margarine
3 tablespoons all-purpose flour
2½ cups milk, or chicken or vegetable stock
1 teaspoon dry mustard
black pepper
¾ cup Cheddar cheese, grated
3 tablespoons grated Parmesan
2–3 tomatoes, peeled and sliced

Freezer standbys for microwaves

- cream — buy in small amounts for easy use and quick thawing
- shrimps — for garnishing or use with other ingredients
- minute steaks
- mixed vegetables — for serving hot or cold
- vol-au-vent cases — for buffets or appetizers
- ice cream — a dependable dessert
- pre-cooked casseroles
- pre-cooked pies
- pre-cooked rice — easy to serve with casseroles or in salads
- flounder fillets — with a sauce or lemon slices
- whole salmon — excellent for last-minute entertaining

If using the oven method (see below), first turn the oven on to 425°F.

Cook the macaroni in plenty of boiling salted water for about 10 minutes until just tender. Drain.

Meanwhile melt the butter and fry the onion and garlic gently until soft. Stir in the herbs, tuna fish and yogurt and heat thoroughly. Season well.

While this is cooking, make the sauce by melting the butter in a pan, stirring in the flour and cooking it for a minute or so. Gradually add the milk or stock and bring it to the boil. Stir in the mustard and salt and pepper, and simmer for two minutes. Add two thirds of the Cheddar and 1 tablespoon of the Parmesan.

Then *either* heat the tuna, macaroni and sauce together for 5 minutes in the pan, pour into a serving dish and lay the tomatoes on top, serving the rest of the cheese to be sprinkled on top, *or,*

if you have more time, put the macaroni in an ovenproof dish, spoon the tuna over it, pour on the sauce, cover with the sliced tomatoes and the rest of the cheese and cook in the preheated oven for 20 minutes.

Feeding a multitude
There may be too many people to sit down to dinner, or it might be that everybody ate in the early evening and you just want to provide a drink and something to soak it up. For either of these the answer is a buffet (see pages 56–9). Determine the amounts of food by the anticipated appetites.

With the exception possibly of a few hot pastries at the outset, keep to cold finger food, such as open-face sandwiches, or you will find you are spending most of the short time of a late-night party in the kitchen. All this cold food should be prepared in advance; wrap the sandwiches in foil, and put the salads in bowls with plastic wrap over the top.

The nightcap
Out of respect to drivers and the next morning's heads, stick to wines with a low alcohol content such as Riesling. White wines in general have less alcohol than red, and their cooler temperature makes for slower absorption of

Pre-prepared open-face sandwiches can solve many of the problems of feeding a large number of people late in the evening. Use a variety of breads for the base, with cold meats, shrimps, cheese slices, cream cheese and sliced hard-boiled eggs for the fillings. The special touch comes with the toppings, of which there can be several on each, providing they complement the other flavors.

the alcohol. Liqueurs are not the easiest of drinks to sleep off, but there are people who swear that whiskey or brandy make ideal nightcaps. If you have bottles on hand, don't deprive them of their happy end to the perfect evening!

Quantities

Working out the amounts of food and drink for large numbers of people is not simply a matter of thinking of how much you would provide for one person and multiplying it by the number invited. For one thing, there is the question of the decreasing quantities consumed per head by increasing numbers of guests (see p.10), and then there are the amounts of uneatable parts of the ingredients, like meat bones, which do not necessarily increase in proportion to the total weight. The following chart gives guidance as to what to provide for 20 or 50 people at a buffet party and can be used to work out quantities for other numbers.

FOOD	20 PORTIONS	50 PORTIONS
Soup	8 pints	18 pints
Pâté	2$\frac{1}{2}$ lb	5 lb
Quiche	4 × 9 inch	10 × 9 inch
Fish (filleted)	5$\frac{1}{2}$ lb	14 lb
Chicken (on the bone)	5 × 3 lb birds, dressed	12 × 3 lb birds, dressed
Meat (cold, sliced) (on the bone) (off the bone)	3$\frac{1}{4}$ lb 7 lb 5 lb	6 lb 16 lb 12 lb
Rice or pasta	3$\frac{1}{4}$ lb	8 lb
Potatoes (for salad)	5 lb	11 lb
Lettuce	3-4	8-9
Cucumber	2	5
Tomatoes	3 lb	7 lb
Italian dressing	1 pint	2$\frac{1}{2}$ pints
Soft fruit (e.g. strawberries)	4 lb	9 lb
Cheese and crackers	2 lb cheese 1$\frac{1}{2}$ lb crackers	4 lb cheese 3 lb crackers
Cheese for main course	4$\frac{1}{2}$ lb	12 lb
Wine	10 regular bottles	20 regular bottles
Hard liquor	3 quarts	7 quarts

Index

Page numbers given in italics refer to illustrations.

ACKNOWLEDGMENTS

The publishers would like to thank the following organizations and individuals for their kind permission to reproduce the photographs in this book:

Ace Photo Agency/Michael Bluestone 42/3, Bill Bachman 2-3, Mauritius Bildagentur 93, Constance Spry Foundation/Martin Brigdale 13, 27, James Jackson 31, 32, 45, 56, Duncan McNicol 101, 114-15, Spike Powell 53, 88-9, 121; Octopus Publishing Group Ltd/Sue Atkinson 91, 95, 105, 107, Jan Baldwin 103, Mike Bales 23, Mick Duff 68-9, Alan Dunns 38-9, Gina Harris 118-19, James Jackson 67, Chris Linton 51, Steve Lyne 61, 64-5, 76, Duncan McNicol 98-9, 109, 110, 113, James Murphy 8-9, 25, 35, 36-7, 79, 86-7, 117, 122-3, Peter Myers 70-71, Clive Streeter 18-19, 29, 46, 63, Paul Williams 14-15, 21, 41, 54, 73, 84-5, 125, Octopus Picture Library 49; Sally and Richard Greenhill 59, 80-81; Susan Griggs Agency/ Sandra Lousada 75, 82, Tony Stone Associates Ltd/ Ron Sutherland 11, 96-7, The Telegraph Colour Library/S. Zarember 6-7, 16-17.

We would also like to thank Rob Shone for the drawings and Eleanor Van Zandt for editorial help.